Fr. Slavko Barbarić, O. F. M.

P[RAY WITH] THE HEART!

Medugorje Manual of Prayer

MEDUGORJE

In accordance with the decree of Pope Urban VIII and Act II of the Vatican Council the writer states that he does not wish to question church authority to which he submits completely.
The words »Apparitions, miracles, messages« and others have, in this case, the value of human testimony.

PUBLISHED IN YUGOSLAVIA BY: PARISH OFFICE

VIGANJ

50267 KUCISTE

English translation: Jozo Kraljević

Published and distributed in the United States by Franciscan University Press, Steubenville, OH 43952
ISBN 0-940535-14-9

TABLE OF CONTENTS

Introduction 5
Practical Instructions 7
Preface 9
Places of Prayer in Međugorje 11

Morning Prayer 13
Evening Prayer 21

Prayer to the Holy Spirit 29

Prayer of Consecration to Our Lady 33

Praying the Rosary 35
a) The Rosary 39
b) The Rosary of Peace 57
c) The Jesus Rosary 63

Prayer before Confession 69

Prayer on Fast Days 77

Adoration of Jesus in the Most Blessed Sacrament . . 81
Adoration of the Holy Cross 91

The Way of the Cross 105

Prayer on the Site of Apparitions 131

Prayer before Mass 135
Thanksgiving after Holy Mass 139

Prayers for Healing 141

When You Return Home 147

INTRODUCTION

Unusual as it may sound, it is at the same time true: our time is a praying time. The people of our time, who are always in a hurry, stop to pray after all. They do so because they feel a primeval need to talk to God, to tell him what they are unable to tell men, not even the closest of friends. For people know that God is the closest and most intimate friend to man after all.

Therefore, dear readers, if you want to be close to and more intimate with our greatest friend, Jesus Christ, then stop and reflect on this book. It will teach you, in a simple way, how to love God and your neighbour, without which love, prayer cannot be fruitful.

This book does not threaten, it does not speak about God's punishment, but about God's love. It calls to us and upon us to be the proud and devout children of God. It calls us, the small, to become great by following Jesus' Gospel. It calls us, who are weary and burdened, to find rest and peace through the power of Jesus' Gospel. It calls us sinners to become holy through Jesus' Gospel.

We have read many books about prayer. Here is finally a book which is a prayer by itself. It does not deal with how it should be prayed, but it is prayed in it as every Christian believer should pray, from heart to heart, from soul to soul, from the painful cry of a miserable man to the merciful response of the God-man.

Rivers and streams of grace flow between us. Year after year. Day after day. Shall we bypass these rivers and streams? Shall we allow these living waters, the waters of mercy, to flow away into the immense abyss of hopelessness? Of course, we are not going to allow

5

something like that. And it is exactly this wonderful spiritual book of the spiritual scientist, Fr. Slavko Barbarić, O. F. M., Ph. D., which, in a wonderful and simple way, speaks of all the beauties of Christian spirituality.

Whoever has read this book, will truly enrich himself spiritually. Whoever accepts this book as a prayer manual, will discover the best prayer-book. And he who accepts it merely as a literary from, will not be disappointed either.

Jakov Bubalo

PRACTICAL INSTRUCTIONS

Morning and Evening Prayers

Beginners can take only one of the seven points of the prayer pattern every day with one Our Father, Hail Mary, Glory Be and the Creed.

Those who feel a greater need of meeting God in prayer will take one of the seven suggested patterns and recite seven Our Fathers, Hail Marys, Glory Bes, and the Creed.

The most advanced will find time to go through all the seven points every day or at least once a week.

The Adoration of the Most Blessed Sacrament

The adoration of the Most Blessed Sacrament has been practiced in Međugorje since 1982, first on the first Thursday in the month and then, since March 1, 1984, on every Thursday after the evening Mass. Groups and individuals can make use of this pattern in their churches whenever they want to. But for everyday visits to Jesus only one point of meditation can suffice.

The Adoration of the Cross

This devotion has been customary in the Međugorje church since 1984, on Fridays after the evening Mass. Elsewhere it can be made according to need, especially during Lent. Its parts, as independent wholes, can also be used individually in everyday life. They are especially recommended to the sick and their attendants.

The Way of the Cross

While you are in Međugorje, you will best experience the way of the cross by climbing Mount Križevac. Likewise, you can make this devotion in any church or chapel, or in your room on Fridays and whenever you want to experience Jesus' Easter message about the meaning of His suffering.

Prayers for Healing

These are regularly said in Međugorje after the evening Mass. They can be used by all who want it, depending on their needs.

Praying the Rosary

Since August 1984 the whole Rosary has been recited in Medugorje: two parts before Mass, the third part after it. If you cannot say the whole Rosary every day, then, according to the common practice in the Church, pray the joyful mysteries on Mondays and Thursdays, the sorrowful mysteries on Tuesdays and Fridays, the glorious mysteries on Wednesdays, Saturdays and Sundays.

The Rosary of Peace and the Jesus Rosary can be prayed according to one's own disposition.

Preface

When you come to Medugorje, you will hear that we are called to prayer, not only to the one in the morning or evening, to the individual or common prayer, but to the prayer with the heart as well.

Every prayer can be finished in haste so that we say all our prayers to the end, without having met Jesus and Mary. If we go on like this, there is a danger of our having only wasted our time, never coming to like prayer. Therefore, it is important to find time for prayer.

In this booklet you will find that Our Lady invites you to prayer in front of the cross and to prayer in front of the Most Blessed Sacrament. She also invites you to confess properly, to prepare yourself properly for Holy Mass and to give thanks after it. You will find messages urging you to devote yourself to God through the Virgin Mary. To devote yourself to God means to decide every day for love, for forgiving, for charity, and against evil and sin, against Satan and all his deeds, as well as against all collaboration with him.

These are the principal thoughts that will lead us through this prayer booklet.

I would certainly like it to be only an incentive. The prayers which follow are the result of an experience. This prayer manual will answer its purpose if it helps you to change over to your personal prayer which will include the same elements.

With the messages which Our Lady used to give on Thursdays and which she now gives on the 25th of every month, she has offered her life of prayer and shown how one grows spiritually.

Everything is directed to the person of Jesus Christ. Our Lady is aware that all her qualities result only from her personal relationship with Jesus Christ. And everything she has advised us has only one aim: to bring us to Jesus.

And to come to Jesus means to touch the life source which gives the water that never runs dry. For Jesus is the model of a man who is at the same time God as well.

These prayers have been woven from a praying experience and have matured with the messages. May they help you, too, dear pilgrim, to come a step closer to Jesus. And he will bring you closer to peace, to love, to reconciliation and togetherness of all people as brothers and sisters, to growing together of God's people into a large family. And exactly such a one gathers in Medugorje from all the four winds: Christ is its head, the Holy Spirit its strength, Mary its mother, and heaven its home.

Only in this way shall we all be able to experience how good it is to be together like brothers and sisters, gathered around the same Mother who leads on and does not stop leading until we all come to our Father's home.

Dear pilgrim, may your coming here be a step closer to all this and finally a preparation for a safe passage to our eternal homeland!

The places of prayer in Međugorje

The apparitions started on Podbrdo, known today as the Hill of Apparitions. Through the force of circumstances they were transferred to houses, then to the parish church, to the rectory, and now to the balcony of the church. From time to time they occurred on Mount Krizevac as well. When the restrictions on movement about the parish at the time of Our Lady's apparitions were lifted, the bud of Medugorje started to develop into a beautiful flower: now the overall experience of Medugorje meetings in the consciousness of most pilgrims includes not only the evening service in the parish church, but also the penitent ascent of the Hill of Apparitions above Bijakovici, and of Krizevac above Medugorje. These three places of prayer certainly form part of the outward spiritual programme as well.

Therefore, when you come to Međugorje, alone or in a group, go into the church and pray! That is the beginning. Pay homage to Jesus! Open your heart to him completely! If you can, go to confession! Start your pilgrim day here! Take part in the Mass of your language group! Give thanks after Mass! And this is the first step you can make in Medugorje. To pray in the church, to meet Jesus like the shepherds in Bethlehem did.

From here start for Križevac, when you can. It is best to set out on foot from the church. No matter whether you go alone or in a group, start praying immediately! It is like the road from Bethlehem to Calvary. When you start climbing up the mountain itself, the stations of the cross wait for you. Make a stop by each and think! In this booklet you will find enough help for it. Take your time, do not hurry! Unite with Jesus! When you reach the top, pray under the Cross, be the weather nice or bad. Take courage! Pray your fullest under the Cross! Cry your heart out because of your sins! Open your heart before the Cross and you will know what it means. In this booklet you will also find a prayer of adoration before the Cross. Pray! Never mind the time! Whoever holds out under the Cross, can go further, receive new assignments and have new experiences.

The view from the Cross opens wide in all directions. Especially it opens towards the Hill of Apparitions, towards Podbrdo. Go to this place, too, and pray! It is not so steep as Križevac, as Calvary, but it is a hill after all. We have become used to learning about meetings on hills from Jesus' life. Before his ascension to heaven he called his disciples together on a hill and then sent them to Jerusalem to pray and from there to the whole world. Open your heart again on the Hill of Apparitions. Here you will sense in a special way how resurrection is close to us, how a road into the world opens to us, waiting for us full of troubles and hardships. Mary appeared on this hill, first with a child in her arms, then with the Cross, too. From here many went home and started doing what the Lord told them.

If you stay for several days, dear pilgrim, do it again. Each time it is a new experience.

Do not look for visionaries, do not bother about shopping. Try to live humbly! Mary educates for new simplicity. But without Bethlehem, without the Cross, without the meeting on the Hill of Mission and without Jerusalem, as places of prayer, we cannot understand what is essential here, nor can we be sent out.

MORNING PRAYER

1. In the name of the Father, and of the Son, and of the Holy Spirit do I begin this day. Father, thank You for having created me just with these characteristics of spirit and body!

Thank You for having created time, which flows and empties into eternity! Thank You for eternity, which does not pass! Thank You for immersing me once into Your immense love and enjoying an untroubled bliss for ever! Thank You for the hope that awakes in me again this morning, for it is going to be my strength for this day with all its troubles, sufferings and problems. I know that nothing is vain for those who are with You, who seek you in everything.

Thank You for the light of this new day, for it helps me to imagine the eternal light that never sets! Therefore, I open myself to the created light in order to attain to the uncreated and eternal light.

Father, thank You for having sent us Your Son Jesus Christ who said of himself: I am the Light of the world, I am the Way to the world, I am the Truth of the world.

Father, thank You for Your Spirit, by whose help I shall be able to live in the Light today, to make progress on the Way and to live the Truth!

This morning, Father, I also thank You for Mother Mary! She is the lodestar of the new day, the dawn of a new daybreak, a Mother clothed with the sun, with the moon at her feet. You showed in her what You offer to us all. Thank You for having created her without sin in the bosom of her mother and for having prepared her immaculate heart as the first abode for Your Son in the Holy Spirit!

Father, grant that I may start this day with joy, in the light of Your love! Grant that I may understand it as Your gift! Help me to live it joyfully in hope! Give me a joyful strength for love, for good deeds, for reconciliation and a permanent longing for You, the spring of pure joy!

(Remain in silence! After a short meditation confide your plans and duties of this day to the Lord!)

Our Father, Hail Mary, Glory Be . . . .

2. Father, thank You for my being able also today to decide for You in all my thoughts, feelings and actions. Now, too, I decide for You as Your Son Jesus Christ decided for You and as his and our Mother decided for You. She invited me, too, in Your name with the following words:

»Dear children! I call upon you to decide for God completely. I beg you, dear children, to abandon yourselves completely to God and you will be able to live all that I am talking about; it will not be difficult for you to surrender to God completely. Thank you for having responded to my call.« (January 2, 1986.)

Father, I decide for You, and pray to You that my decision may be permanent, that You may, also today, have the first place for me in every situation, that I may also today seek Your glory and live Your love. I pray especially to You that I may withstand all the trials of the day: do not allow my love and my devotion to be weak!

I pray to You, Lord, for those I shall meet today that they will decide to live for You devotedly. Then my devotion will be easier, too. May my devotion and my decision of this morning be a support and an encouragement to others.

14

(Recommend by name those whom you know you are going to meet today!)

Our Father, Hail Mary, Glory be . . .

3. Father, thank You that by my decision and devotion I belong to You today and forever! I know, Father, that both in me and in the world there is still a lot of evil and sin. I know that the Prince of Darkness (the Archenemy of men from the beginning, the Seducer and the Deceiver, Satan) is not idle but seduces and destroys love and peace. Therefore, now, at the beginning of this day I consciously decide for You, and against Satan. I renounce all his seductions. I break off every collaboration with him.

Father, thank You for having given me freedom and for my being able to decide for You of my own free will! Thank You that Your Son and our Saviour Jesus exposed the action of evil and conquered it by the strength of his love and sacrifice! Thank You, Father, not only for having preserved Mary from sin and the effect of evil, but also for having made her our mighty intercessor!

Mary, this morning I want to respond to the call which you address to all:

»Dear children! I invite each of you to start living in God's love. Dear children, you are ready to commit sin, and to give yourselves up into the hands of Satan thoughtlessly. I invite each of you to decide for God consciously, and against Satan. I am your mother. Therefore, I want to lead you all to complete holiness. I want each of you to be with me in heaven. This is, dear children, the purpose of my coming here, and my wish. Thank you for having responded to my call!« (May 25, 1987)

Mary, this morning I really want to respond to your call. I am sorry that I am still inclined to commit sin, that I still do not love as I should, that there are still moments when earthly things are more important to me than the

15

spiritual ones. I am sorry that my words are not always very kind, that my thoughts are sometimes unchaste.

I do not want to sin any more. I renounce sin. I renounce every unconscious collaboration with evil. If there is anything left in me that serves sin and that gives me up thoughtlessly into the hands of the enemy of my spirit, soul and body, the enemy of my life, now I renounce it deliberately. With you, O Mary, I pray for the favour of being aware of all my actions, that all my actions may be in the service of goodness, love, peace and reconciliation.

(Think of your evil habits and sins and renounce them quite concretely, mentioning them by name!)

Our Father, Hail Mary, Glory Be . . .

4. Father, You created me in such a way as to be able, only through my love for You and my neighbours, to become happy here on earth and come into heavenly, eternal happiness. Therefore I renounce every dislike, every hatred, all bad ways, every blasphemy, either of mine or of others, and decide for LOVE. Send me Your Spirit that I may love You as Your Son Jesus Christ loved You! Give me love that I may love You in all men and in all creatures! Thank You that Your Son Jesus Christ gave his life for me out of love! That is why today, in spite of all my sins, I cry for joy: Father, I want to love You!

Thank You for having made Mary, the Mother, a mother of goodness, love and mercy! Thank You that she wants to educate us for love towards You and towards all men!

Mary, thank You for being so tireless in the effort to teach us love! Thank you for this call:

»Dear children, today I invite you to live the words I LOVE GOD this week! Dear children, by love you shall achieve everything, even what you think impossible. God wants this parish to belong completely to Him. And that is what I want, too. Thank you for having responded to my call!« (February, 28, 1985)

Mary, at your motherly word I decide: I shall live love for God every moment of this day. O Mother of love, teach me love and pray for love with me!

Mary, I pray to you now for all those I shall work and live with today that they may live your message as well. Let my decision be a help to them, as their decision will help me!

(Mention by name those you will meet, you work with and you work for, that there may be love in everything!)

Our Father, Hail Mary, Glory Be . . .

5. Father, You wanted me to be born into a family, too. At the beginning of this day I thank You for my family, for every member of my close and distant relatives! Without them I would be lonesome, forsaken, no orderly life and work would be impossible for me. Therefore, Father, thank You for their love towards me, because it comes from You! Thank You for all good and nice things I experienced in my family and with my dear ones!

(Mention them by name!)

I decide personally for love in my family and I would like to love them all as You love us all. I also pray to You for the families of my brothers, and sisters, of all my relatives, and for all families in the world. Father, to Your love I commend all those who have remained without love and peace, because sin has destroyed them. Give them back the strength for love and peace! Heal their wounds! Make them happy!

Mary, Mother of our families, thank you for having lived in the holy family and shown that it is possible to live togetherness and love. Intercede for us and pray for our families! Thank you for being our teacher in this message as well:

»Dear children! You know that the time of joy is approaching, and without love you will achieve nothing. Therefore, first start loving your family, all your parishioners, and then you will be able to accept and love all those who come here! Let this week be a time for you to learn how to love. Thank you for having responded to my call!« (December 13, 1984)

Refresh me personally and protect my decisions with your motherly mantle! Grant that today in my family love may be the principal rule of behaviour between each other! Let love, through your intercession, heal all wounds from yesterday, and let joy make its abode in us!

Our Father, Hail Mary, Glory Be . . .

6. Father, this morning I thank You especially for the grace to co-operate in building the world with the gifts You gave me. Ahead of me is a day given in gift by Your grace. I want to do everything for Your glory, for my own good and for the good of all people. Teach me so that my work today is a continuation of this morning's prayer!

Bless my family at work, the community and the whole world! Bless all those who work today, but also those who do not work because they are unemployed or do not know how to find employment! Hire them all in Your vineyard to build a better world! Do not allow us to overwork! Refresh the tired, inspire the artists, open to inventors an approach to new possibilities of the laws You put into Your creatures! Grant that everything praises and glorifies You.

18

You, Father, sent Your Son to teach us how to work. And all He did was for Your greater glory. Let Him enrich us with His Spirit that we may keep the balance between manual labour and mental work!

Mary, our Mother, thank you for having called us to turn to the Creator in our work and to ask His blessing before and after every work!

»Dear children! Today I want to tell you to pray before starting to work and to finish your work with prayer. If you do so, God will bless both you and your work. These days you have been praying little and working much. So pray! You will find rest in prayer. Thank you for having responded to my call!« (July 5, 1984)

Thank you for your motherly call. Mother Mary, pray with me to the Father that he may forgive me for having so many times forgotten to ask for His fatherly blessing. May he forgive me for having often considered myself as the master, forgetting that I am only the administrator of the goods entrusted to me, and for having so often misused my working abilities! Mother, let me become a good co-operator with God's plans! Mary, pray to the Father that He may forgive all for having sometimes destroyed themselves both with overwork and idleness! Let all people consciously and joyfully work together in building the world, and let everybody's work today be blessed!

Our Father, Hail Mary, Glory Be . . .

7. Father, now in this prayer I have opened my heart before You and nourished my soul to the full. Refresh both my soul and body that I may be able to fulfill my task! Here I am, Father! I repeat this word with Your Son Jesus Christ for all nice and hard moments that lie in store for me today. I pronounce the words: I am the

19

servant of the Lord, like Mary, the Mother of Your Son, did.

Mary, thank You for helping me to understand that I am also important for the salvation of the world, that I, too, can bring peace and love!

»Dear children! I invite you to be an example to others in everything, especially in prayer and testifying! Dear children, I cannot help the world without you. I want you to co-operate with me in everything, even in the least things! So, dear children, help me that your prayer may come from the heart and that you all may give yourselves up to me completely! In this way I shall be with you. Thank you for having responded to my call!« (August 28, 1986)

The servant of God, I am ready to respond and come with you to help the world. Thank you that want to be with me and that I am important to you! Thank you for the words that you cannot help the world without me. Let me understand, like you did, the Father's plan for me today! Amen!

Our Father, Hail Mary, Glory Be . . .

Trusting in You, Father, I repeat with the Church that I believe in You and that I confide my heart to You:

I believe in God . .

EVENING PRAYER

1. Father, the day has passed and the evening has come. I pray to You to send me Your Spirit that I may in Your light, consciously spend these moments which I want to devote to You and to myself! Thank You for being ready to listen to me as Your child!

Father, hush my heart as the heart of a child is hushed in its father's bosom! Hush my heart at the sunset of this day as a baby is hushed in its mother's bosom! As everything around me is falling into the darkness of the night, send me Your light which never passes! Appease my soul as a doe is appeased at a water spring and as the earth is appeased after a fruitful rain!

Mary, so many times did You hush Jesus, Your son, as a child in your motherly bosom and commit Him to the calm of the night. So I, too, ask you to be with me in these moments, that peace and appeasement may enter into my heart, that they may affect my soul and body.

Mary, thank You for having called me to change my heart. You said:

»**Dear children! I would like to tell you today to start working on your hearts like you work in your fields. Work and change your hearts that a new spirit from God may settle down in them. Thank you for having responded to my call!**« (April 25, 1985)

(Remain in silence and open to peace!)

Our Father, Hail Mary, Glory Be . . .

2. Father, I have worked today and gotten tired. Thank You for my having had a chance to make use of the gifts You gave for my own good and for the good of others. Thank You that I have been hard-working today, too. And now I pray to You to give me grace to cultivate my heart,

as I was ready to do other jobs during the day! Father, I pray to You that I may, at Mary's intercession, redecorate and cultivate my heart, that it may change and become good and pure! Remove from it the dust of sin and evil. Let a new Spirit make its abode in me! Father, I admit: I have sinned today, too. At times selfishness and haughtiness took hold of me. I was angry and impatient. Others around me have sinned, too, uttering blasphemies, curses, lies and slanders ... Father, all this has burdened my heart. So, cleanse and wash me! Cleanse my consciousness and subconsciousness that peace may settle down in me!

Mary, thank you for your call to cleanse ourselves of sin:

»Dear children! Today, too, I invite you to prepare your hearts for all the days when the Lord especially wants to cleanse you of all sins from your past. You, dear children, are not able to do it alone. That is why I am here to help you. Pray, dear children! Only in this way will you be able to recognize all the evil that is in you and to deliver it to the Lord in order that He may completely cleanse your hearts. So, dear children, pray without ceasing and prepare your hearts in penance and fasting! Thank you for having responded to my call!« (December 4, 1986)

Mary, thank you for being here to help us to cleanse ourselves! O Mother, take me on your lap now! A mother makes little of how much her child is dirty and soiled, she rather helps it to be clean and nice. Do so with me now! Let the Lord, at your intercession, take the burdens from my heart!

(Remain again in silence!)

Our Father, Hail Mary, Glory Be ...

3. Father, now I pray to You for my family.

(Mention the members of your family by name or the members of your community!)

Let none of us go to the night's rest, burdened with the sins of the day! You know us well. Thank You for not condemning us but for giving us also, at the end of this day, the grace to cleanse ourselves and so to be able again to meet tomorrow and work together for Your glory! Heal the wounds we inflicted on each other by insufficient love, mistrust, slander! Father, cleanse and calm each one of us that peace may flourish tomorrow!

(Pray especially for the person you may have quarrelled and argued with, who hurt you and left a wound in you! Do this in silence!)

Mary, help through your motherly intercession my family and my community! Help all families to enjoy the night's peace with you in the Lord! Mary, thank you for the words with which you called us to inner beauty, when you said:

»Dear children! Once again today I want to invite you to pray. When you pray, dear children, you become more like flowers which, after the snow, show forth their beauty, and all their colors become indescribable. And so you, dear children, after prayer before God, display everything that is beautiful so that you may become beloved by Him. Therefore, dear children, pray and open your inner self to the Lord so that He may make of you a harmonious and beautiful flower for heaven. Thank you for having responded to my call!« (December 18, 1986)

Mary, Mother of goodness, love and mercy, Mother full of divine beauty, let our family become a new wonderful flower! Let the ice of misunderstanding disappear from our family and from all families! Let everybody open and confide his inner self to you, like a child confides in its mother! Mary, thank you for being ready to be our mother, although many times we have refused to co-operate with your calls! From now on we want to be beautiful and show all the beatuy of colours given to us. Grant that we

23

may become endeared to each other, and, all together with you, to the Lord!

Our Father, Hail Mary, Glory Be . . .

4. Father, thank You for giving me back my peace, for healing my wounds and the wounds of my family! Thank You for delivering me from the burden of the day that I may immerse myself into a deep peace and regain strength for the new day and the new co-operation with You in the world! But before I close my eyes, my thoughts go also to those of Your children, and my brothers and sisters, who cannot have a peaceful sleep, because they are burdened. Therefore, I pray to You with Mary, the Mother of Your Son and the Mother of us all, that they may find peace, too. You know that hatred breaks families and communities, so that many are on the streets now, abondoned, despised, seeking consolation in alcohol and drugs, in dissipated life, but peace they do not find, nor is consolation given to them. Only new wounds are open- ed and a new grief reigns in hearts and families. Father, I pray to You for them. I especially include the young and children who do not find rest nor repose because their parents are at odds with each other. Mary, I pray for them together with you, for you said:

»**Dear children I invite you again to prayer with the heart. If you pray with your heart, dear children, the ice cold hearts of your brothers will melt and all obstacles will disappear. Conversion will be easy for all those who want to receive it. It is a gift you have to obtain by prayer for your neighbour. Thank you for having respon- ded to my call.**« (January 23, 1986)

Mary, all men are my neighbours. So, at your word I pray to the Lord that all obstacles to peace and appease- ment may disappear. May all be converted and saved! Let the spring of joy and togetherness come to all men!

(Recommend in silence somebody who you know is in restlessness and anxiety!)

Our Father, Hail Mary, Glory Be . . .

5. Father, now I direct my thoughts to those who cannot enter into a peaceful sleep and who do not find appeasement in their heart, because they are weighed down with illness or attend the sick. I pray to You with an honest heart for them, too.

Look upon all the sick in our families and in our hospitals! Who can appease and soothe their heart if not You, Lord of all hearts? Alleviate their wounds and pains! Give them love that they could bear their pains, like Your Son bore His cross! Father, I pray to You for Your sick children and my sick brothers and sisters. Grant Your grace to all who suffer from mental or physical pains that they may present their crosses for their own salvation and the salvation of the world! Let them feel also in this moment that You accept their sacrifices!

Bless especially those who nurse the sick! Let their love for the sick be inexhaustible! Send them rest and peace by the gift of love that comes from You!

Mary, faithful Mother! You did not run away from the cross of your Son but remained loyal to the end. Let all those who cannot find a peaceful rest now feel that you are by them! Obtain grace for them through prayer that they may offer their sacrifices to God, as you called us all:

»Dear children! I thank you for every sacrifice you have offered! I again urge you to offer each sacrifice with love. I want you, the helpless, to start helping with confidence, and the Lord will give to you in confidence. Thank you for having responded to my call!« (July 4, 1985)

Mary, thank you for these words! Let them echo in the hearts of all the sick and infirm, of all who suffer in one way or another! Mother of consolation, obtain grace for them by prayer that they may understand with the heart this word of yours and constantly offer themselves as a living sacrifice of love for salvation! You know how pain and suffering can exhaust and take away all inner strength. So obtain through your prayers peace and appeasement for them.

(Recommend especially a sick person you know!)

Our Father, Hail Mary, Glory Be . . .

6. Father, I cannot go to my sleep without praying to You, sincerely and from my heart, for all those who are at war now, who persecute and destroy each other by modern weapons. Father, forgive us for having misused the achievements and the laws You allowed us to discover to make weapons and means of destruction! You wanted them to serve us for the good. Father, forgive our wars and conflicts! Heal the hearts of all who are deceived and exploited, who are persecuted and deprived of their rights, that peace may come to a world which thirsts after it!

Father, give back peace to those who in their hearts bear the need for violence and revenge! Open the way of peace to every heart. Send them Your light to make them aware of all lies and deceit so that nobody ever becomes a victim of their violence again!

Enlighten with Your light all statesmen, all parliaments, all those who decide about the destiny of the world! Let them bow down before You, let them recognize You as the Lord! Let them work for peace, let them understand that every authority is given from You as a gift for service! Father, let us understand that peace is not for us only or for our friends, but for all people! O, let peace come!

Mary, Queen and Mother of Peace, obtain through prayers, peace for each of your children, for each family! At your word I pray now before the cross for peace, for you said:

»Dear children! There is no peace without prayer. So I tell you, dear children, to pray for peace in front of the cross. Thank you for having responded to my call!« (September 6, 1984)

(Remain kneeling for a while in front of the cross and mention in words the unreconciled! Then pray!)

Our Father, Hail Mary, Glory Be . . .

7. Father, at the end of my prayer this evening I ask You for Your blessing. Bless me with the blessing of peace, love and reconciliation! Bless me that I may grow while my body is at rest. Bless me that my love may be alive while my body and soul are overcome by sleep! Let the seed of Your word grow in me, through Your blessing, while I am asleep! Let it grow irrepressibly both in my family and in the whole world.

Mary, Mother of goodness and love, Mother of God's word! Be by me and by your every child! Drive away every evil and every influence of evil from me and from all people! Obtain by prayer, together with me, the blessing you invited us all to when you said:

»Dear children! I would like to invite you to grow in love. A flower cannot normally grow without water. Neither can you, dear children, grow without God's blessing. You should seek God's blessing from day to day so that you may grow normally and do everything with God. Thank you for having responded to my call!« (April 10, 1986)

Here, Mary, I am asking for a blessing with you. Obtain it by prayer from God for me in all its fullness!

Our Father, Hail Mary, Glory Be . . .

Father, at the end I give my heart over to You and pray confessing my faith in You, the Triune God, Father, Son and Holy Spirit.

I believe . . .

PRAYER TO THE HOLY SPIRIT

Mary, thank you for having called me to pray every day to the Holy Spirit through whom you conceived Jesus Christ, through whom you in meditation understood the word of God and remained faithful to it to the end.

»Dear children! This evening I would like to tell you to pray in the days of this Novena for the outpouring of the Holy Spirit on your families and on your parish. Pray! You shall not regret it. God shall give you the gifts with which you will praise him to the last breath of your life on earth. Thank you for having responded to my call!« (June 2, 1984)

O Spirit, I pray to You now with Mary who called me to pray to You. Pour Yourself out on me with all Your gifts!

Pour out the gift of love into my life that from now on I may love God in You above all, and my neighbour as myself.

Pour out on me the gift of wisdom that I may – in everything I do and think, feel and decide – always think, decide and act in Your light.

O Spirit of Counsel, descend on me that I may, with my knowledge and the word of love, help those who ask me for counsel! Let my every word be a light to others!

Spirit of Jesus, grant me the gift of Your strength that I may stand every trial and do the Father's will, especially in times of hardship! Spirit of fortitude, strengthen me in the hours of frailty!

O Spirit of life, develop divine life within me which was given to me through You already in the bosom of my mother and at my baptism!

Divine fire, inflame the fire of divine love in my heart

so that the darkness and ice of sin may disappear from it!

Spirit of healing, heal within me all that is wounded, and develop the undeveloped!

Descend on me with all Your strength that I may be thankful for small things as well. Enlighten me, Holy Spirit, that I may know how to appreciate crosses and hardships, too.

Mary, you are the bearer of the Holy Spirit. So thank you for calling me to pray for the Spirit of truth.

»Dear children! Tomorrow evening pray for the Spirit of truth. Especially you from the parish. For you need the Spirit of truth that you convey the messages as they are, without adding to or taking away anything from them, just the way I put them. Pray that the Holy Spirit may inspire you with the spirit of prayer, that you may pray more! I, your Mother, tell you that you pray little. Thank you for having responded to my call!« (June 9, 1984)

O Spirit of truth, enlighten me with Your truth that I may first live the truth of love, peace and righteousness. Help me that I may be able, with my words and deeds, to proclaim every day the Word of the Father in its full light to everybody!

Holy Spirit, guide our Pope, bishops, priests and all others who proclaim the Word of God! Fall on the parish community of Međugorje, too, that it may be able to live Our Lady's messages and to convey them to all! Fall on the priests who preach in Međugorje! Fall on the confessors and those who confess.

Spirit of prayer, teach us how to pray. Cleanse our hearts that we may pray worthily and always find time for prayer! Holy Spirit, pray within me and invoke: Abba, Father! Grant me the favour of praying with the heart!

Mary, I also want to open my heart to the Holy Spirit, as you opened yours when you called me:

»Dear children! These days I invite you especially to open your hearts to the Holy Spirit. These days the Holy Spirit acts through you in a special way. Open your hearts and abandon your life to Jesus that He may act through your hearts and strengthen your faith! Thank you for having responded to my call!« (May 23, 1985)

Holy Spirit, take away all burdens from me that my heart may be like a developing and growing flower that brings abundant fruit! Mary, may the Holy Spirit start and continue within me the deed which started in you, that the divine word may grow within me through it!

O Holy Spirit, through Mary I choose You today the Master of my whole being. With trust and hope in Your endless love, which manifested itself so marvelously in Mary, I decide for You gifts. I renounce every evil spirit and his action, and accept You, Spirit of light, love, peace and order. I devote to You all mybilities and want to act in Your light. I surrender to You all rights over my life. Watch over me and lead me to the Father! I pray to You with Mary through Jesus Christ. Amen.

PRAYER OF CONSECRATION TO OUR LADY

(To be prayed on Our Lady's feasts)

»Dear children! Today again I invite you to devote your life to me with love that I may be able to lead you with love. I love you, dear children, with a special love and I want to bring you all to heaven, to God. I want you to understand that this life is so short compared to that one in heaven. So, dear children, decide for God again today. Only then shall I be able to show you how dear you are to me and how much I wish you were all saved and in heaven with me. Thank you for having responded to my call!« (November 27, 1986)

Mary, thank you for this motherly call! Mother of my Saviour and Mother of Peace, today I surrender my life to you with love. As Jesus, dying on the cross, gave you also over to me, so do I give myself over to you now. Take me on your motherly lap! I want to love Jesus as you did, Mother. I want to learn with you how to listen to the Father's word and do his will.

Mary with you I wish to learn how to love all people as my brothers and sisters because they are all yours. I devote myself to you that my prayer may be prayer of the heart in which I shall find peace, and love, and the strength of reconciliation. To you, Our Lady, do I give up my past, my present and my future, all my abilities and gifts. I want to grow up with you like Jesus did. Let everything in me praise the Lord with you from now on! Let my soul from now on sing for joy to His love and mercy! I dedicate to you, Mother, my family, too, all my friends, all those I live and work with . . .

Mary, I would like to be the bearer of the Holy Spirit with you. Let my heart be obedient to His inspirations, as was yours!

Mother of Peace, let my words be irrevocable through your intercession that sin may never seduce me again! Amen.

PRAYING THE ROSARY

In all her apparitions Our Lady called to prayer. She did not ask for new forms, nor did she offer them. She rather asked for old forms to be renewed and to be given a new life force.

Such is the case with Međugorje, too. At the beginning she suggested seven Our Fathers, Hail Marys and Glory Bes, and the Creed as the minimum of daily prayer. Then she called for one part of the Rosary and finally for all three parts. On the eve of the big feast of her Assumption, August 14, 1984, Our Lady said through Ivan Dragičević:

I would like the world to pray with me these days. Pray all the more. Fast strictly on Wednesdays and Fridays; pray at least the Rosary every day: joyful, sorrowful and glorious mysteries...

Meaning of the Rosary

To recite the Rosary does not mean anything else but to find a way to be with Jesus and Mary.

By meditating on the mysteries of their life, we are with them: be it the joy of Christmas and the seriousness of the presentation in the temple, or sorrow and bloody sweat on the face, the wounds on the back from the scourge and the cross, the crown of thorns on the head. When we are daily linked with them by such meetings, then the joy of victory over death and sin is guaranteed to us with them. The gifts of the Spirit and the final triumph in heaven are assured us.

So, to recite the Rosary does not mean to hide oneself somewhere in a corner and to live far from the world and life. It means to prepare oneself for one's own and other people's crosses, the way Jesus and Mary carried them. To be with them means to have troubles and problems, and yet never to be embittered. To be with them means to experience contempt and disappointment, and yet never to ask for revenge. To go with them means to go the way of a man who believes in God who makes everything new.

Every prayer can be finished in a hasty manner so that we say all our prayers to the end without having met Jesus and Mary. If we do this, there is danger of it becoming a waste of time for us and of our never coming to like prayer. It is just like meeting a friend. If we never have time for him or if the time we devote to him is too short, or if we speak with bad grace, then the friendship is bound to die.

Therefore, it is important **to have time for the prayer of the Rosary and for every prayer.**

Here you will find the prayer of the Rosary (joyful, sorrowful and glorious mysteries) with biblical texts and some personal prayers. Then we give an example of the Rosary for Peace and of the Jesus Rosary.

Before starting to pray, remember Our Lady's messages about the Rosary. Here are some of them:

»Dear children! Today I would like to ask you to make me happy with your prayers again and again. Unfortunately there are a lot of those in the parish who do not pray, and my heart is sad. So pray that I may take all your sacrifices and prayers to the Lord! Thank you for having responded to my call!« (October 4,1984)

»Dear children! Intend all your evening prayers at home for the conversion of sinners because the world is in great sin! Recite the Rosary every evening!« (October 8, 1984 – through Jakov who was ill)

»I call on you to invite everybody to the prayer of the Rosary! By the Rosary you will conquer all the calamities which Satan wants to inflict upon the Catholic Church. Pray the Rosary, all you priests! Devote your time to the Rosary!«

(A message for priests on the anniversary of June 25, 1985 as an answer to the question of Marija Pavlović: »Our Lady, what would you like to recommend to priests?«)

Dear children! Today I invite you in a particular way to enter the battle against Satan by means of prayer. Satan wants to battle more, now that you are aware of his activity. Dear children, put on, therefore, the armour against Satan, and with the Rosary in your hands you will defeat him. Thank you for your response to my call!« (August 8, 1985)

»Dear children! Today I invite you to start praying the Rosary with a living faith. Only in this way shall I be able to help you. You, dear children, want to get favours without praying. In that case I cannot help you because you do not care to move. Dear children, I call on you to pray the Rosary and to accept it as an obligation which you will meet with delight! In doing so you will understand why I have remained so long with you. I want to teach you how to pray. Thank you for having responded to my call!« (June 12, 1986)

THE ROSARY

THE JOYFUL MYSTERIES:
JESUS ENTERS INTO MY LIFE

INTRODUCTORY PRAYER: My Lord and my God, I want to devote to You this time of mine. Quiet my heart. Help me to abandon myself completely to You. Do not let any of my words be empty. Let each be a step closer to You. Enlighten my mind and open my heart so that Your Word may grow within me as a seed of love, faith and hope; that it may grow like it did in the immaculate bosom of the Virgin after she, in all humbleness, had accepted to be the handmaid of God. Help me that I also may place myself at Your disposal as Your faithful servant. I believe in You, Father, in Your Son, and in Your Holy Spirit. Amen.

(Now first I say the Creed and then read or listen to the Biblical words of the prophet Isaiah.)

»Listen, O house of David! is it not enough for you to weary men, must you also weary my God? Therefore the Lord himself will give you this sign: the virgin shall be with child, and bear a son, and shall name him Emmanuel. He shall be living on curds and honey by the time he learns to reject the bad and choose the good.« (Is 7, 13–15)

(There follows now a passage from the Gospel according to Luke.)

»In the sixth month, the angel Gabriel was sent from God to a town of Galilee named Nazareth, to a virgin betrothed to a man named Joseph, of the house of David. The virgin's name was Mary. Upon arriving the angel said to her: 'Rejoice, O highly favoured daughter! The Lord is with you. Blessed are you among women.' She was deeply troubled by his words, and wondered what his greeting meant. The angel went on to say to her: 'Do not fear, Mary. You have found favour with God. You shall conceive and bear a son and give him the name Jesus . . . The Holy Spirit will come upon you and the power of the Most High will overshadow you; hence, the holy offspring to be born will be called Son of God.' . . . 'I am the servant of the Lord. Let it be done to me as you say.'«

Mary! You readily agreed to be the servant of the Lord after having first been troubled and then thought about the heavenly call. Mary! You are the virgin the prophet Isaiah speaks about. You knew your God so well and walked is his presence. You gave him your life because you were awaiting the promised Saviour. You were not troubled because you were not ready to do his will, but because you could not believe that you were exactly the virgin upon whom the power of the Holy Spirit would come and who would bear Emmanuel, »God with us.« Your fear was not the fear of haughty and selfish men, but the fear of God's humble ones who always readily do God's will, but without self-praise and boasting.

Mary! No wonder you were excited because the night of damnation and the night of salvation and the long awaited dawn bearing the Day, met in you.

Mary! Maybe when you had other life plans, God entered into your life with his special plan. And you, as his lowly servant, opened wide the door of your heart to Him. Your example prompts me to turn to the Lord myself and to say to him: Come, O lord! Come, my soul is awaiting You generously and my heart is ready to welcome You. Come into my dreams and into my plans, into my hopes and my fears. Enter into my life and I shall be Your servant all my life. I know that I am not worthy to have You under my roof, but I also know that You love sinners and that You constantly search for them. Therefore, O Lord, enter into my darkness, into my hardships and pains. Enter into where You have been expelled by sin. Enter also into those parts of my life where I preferred my own to Your holy will. Enter now while I am meditating and praying before the cross of Your Son and before the figure of his Mother who conceived him by the power of the Holy Spirit.

(Now one Our Father, ten Hail Marys and at the end one Glory Be are meditatively recited. The following prayer is usually added after each mystery: »O my Jesus, forgive us our sins, save us from the fires of hell, and lead all souls to heaven, especially those who have most need of Your mercy!)

THE SECOND JOYFUL MYSTERY: Mary, you went to visit your cousin Elisabeth. It is God's will that we bring Jesus into the life of other people once he has entered into our life, to bring him into other people's joys and sorrows, into other people's darknesses and bitternesses. Therefore, Mary, let my love for the sick grow and become so strong that I may be able to recognize your Son in every sick brother and sister.

(There follows the Our Father, 10 Hail Marys, Glory Be and the invocation »O my Jesus . . .«)

THE THIRD JOYFUL MYSTERY: Mary, you are the Bearer of the Word and the Mother of salvation. You, who consented to be the servant, become a Mother now. The Lord raises the lowly and that is why you are the Mother of the Saviour. You gave birth to the one whom the prophets had announced and for whom the upright had longed. God has entered into my life, too. I also said, »God, I am Your servant.« But the fruits of my serving have made me neither a brother nor a sister, neither a father nor a mother to people yet. O Mother of my God, grant that he may completely enter into my life while I am adoring Him.

(Our Father, 10 Hail Marys, Glory Be, »O my Jesus . . .«).

THE FOURTH JOYFUL MYSTERY: Mary! I am watching you in my mind now present your first-born Son to the heavenly Father so that salvation may come through him. At the presentation you were certainly saying: »O God, here is my Son. He is the fruit of my womb but he belongs to You, as I want to belong to You with all my heart.« I am also standing with you, Mary, in the temple before the Lord and presenting myself to him following your example. I have received everything, and I give away everything. I do not want to keep anything for myself, either before God or before men.

(Our Father, 10 Hail Marys, Glory Be, »O my Jesus . . .«)

THE FIFTH JOYFUL MYSTERY: I watch you, Mary, bringing up your Son with all responsibility. You had taken him to the temple. The joy of the meeting in the temple turned into a big sorrow for you. For three days you did not know where your Son was and you were unhappy. But your sorrow did not prevent you from doing the Father's will. You went in search of him and your search was rewarded with a new joy.

Mary, while praying these mysteries I am meditating on how God, after having entered into your life, prepares you for ever greater sacrifices and grants you ever greater favours. Encouraged by these mysterious events, I say once again, in face of all trials and fears, »Here I am, O Lord, enter into my life. I want to do Your will, even in times of hardships. I want all my crosses and difficulties to bear new meetings with You.

(Our Father, 10 hail Marys, Glory Be, »O my Jesus . . .«)

CLOSING PRAYER: Thank You, Lord, for my having been able to meditate on Your entering into Mary's life and thank You for having prepared her to receive You. And You did great things in her life, indeed. I know that You are not going to leave me either, for You have entered into my life. Guide me and give me the grace of letting myself be guided. May it be so. Amen.

THE SORROWFUL MYSTERIES:
JESUS GOES WITH ME THROUGH SUFFERING

Father, Your will be done!
In the name of . . .

INTRODUCTORY PRAYER: My Jesus, Your coming to this world was wonderful. Wonderful because You were ready to suffer like all men. You were not spared from crosses, yet You were always ready to alleviate other people's pains, to take crosses away, to heal and to comfort. Now a special hour has come. Your personal Calvary is approaching. Death inevitable is approaching. I do not want either to doze or to sleep, but to stay awake with You. I wish, Jesus, my prayer could bring You comfort in brothers and sisters who suffer. I wish it could bring You joy and strength in them. Send me Your Spirit that I may know how to pray, that I may come closer to You. Amen.

I believe . . .

THE FIRST SORROWFUL MYSTERY: Jesus, You experienced sorrow and distress in the Garden of Gethsemani. You asked Your Father to let the bitter cup pass You by, but You added immediately, »Father, Your will be done!« You who had refreshed many a sufferer found Yourself in suffering alone. There was nobody to help You. The Father could have, but You agreed to drink the bitter cup to the last drop. But it must have been an all too bitter agony to make You sweat with blood. I believe that all the agony and all the suffering of the world was present in Your bloody sweat. Jesus, thank You for every drop of blood that ran with the sweat. I know that from that moment all the agony of the world became an agony that redeems and an agony that can redeem. I pray to You to look upon all those who are seeking the Father's will now, for the sake of Your sweat. Help also those who have learnt the Father's will, but are too weak to accept it. May all the agony be redeemed through a renewed acceptance of the Father's will!

(I remain in silence praying for those who suffer.)

Jesus, open my heart now that I am going to read Luke's account of Your agony!

»Then he went out and made his way, as was his custom, to the Mount of Olives; his disciples accompanied him. On reaching the place he said to them, »Pray that you may not be put to the test«. He withdrew from them about a stone's throw, then went down on his knees and prayed in these words, »Father, if it is your will, take this cup from me; yet not my will but yours be done.« An angel then appeared to him from heaven to strengthen him. In his anguish he prayed with all the greater intensity, and his sweat became like drops of blood falling to the ground. Then he rose from prayer and came to his disciples, only to find them asleep, exhausted with grief. He said to them, »Why are you sleeping? Wake up and pray that you may not be subjected to the trial.« (Lk 22, 39–46)

(Our Father, 10 Hail Marys, Glory Be, »O my Jesus . . .«)

THE SECOND SORROWFUL MYSTERY: Jesus, You were scourged at Pilate's court. I know what the custom was like with scourging: they would tie the condemned person to a post. Then the scourgers would deal unmerciful lashes on the body of the condemned person. My Jesus, this act, too, takes my breath away. My heart freezes . . . However, You magnanimously forgave Your scourgers all the blows with which they wounded You all over. Therefore I pray to You to set free with Your scourges also those who do not want to do the Father's will and who destroy themselves with the scourges which befall them, because they do not decide for forgiveness and love. Thank You for the example of love and forgiveness which manifested itself when they scourged You severely!

(Our Father, 10 Hail Marys, Glory Be, »O my Jesus . . .«)

THE THIRD SORROWFUL MYSTERY: My Jesus, they crowned You with the crown of thorns after the scourging. They wrapped You in a scarlet military cloak and made a fool of You – those who were near You. For, Your friends were far away! When hatred starts forging evil plans, then it is not likely to stop. It was not enough for them to have scourged You so murderously and now they go on mocking You and crowning You with the crown of thorns. But this time, too, hatred and evil were surprised before You. You remained calm in all Your suffering. They saw in Your behaviour that You understood even those who treated You like that. And even more: that You loved them and that You did not condemn them. But their wickedness had no limits. That is what happens when evil has affected a man, a family, a community. Then it never stops destroying. Jesus, look upon all the offended and the humiliated, the scorned and the rejected. Redeem them with Your crown of thorns from under the grindstone of torturers and oppressors. Cleanse their heart of every hatred. Do not let them plan revenge and return evil with evil. Jesus, in Your name, let forgiveness spread!

(Our Father, 10 Hail Marys, Glory Be, »O my Jesus . . .«)

THE FOURTH SORROWFUL MYSTERY: Jesus, You carried Your cross to Calvary. All I know about Your way of the cross is that it was horrifying. However, in a sea of pain and suffering You had three precious drops of consolation: the meeting with Your Mother, Veronica's handkerchief and the brief hand in carrying the cross from Simon the Cyrenean. You certainly appreciated these drops of consolation and rewarded them with consolation and strength. But You may well have wondered at that moment, »Where are the rest whom I have helped so unselfishly? And I know again, You understood them too, and presented Your cross for them as well. Help me, Jesus, to learn something, to be sensitive to other people's pain, to know how to comfort even in the most difficult moments . . . that I may never find it hard to shoulder the burden of others. I especially ask You to help us not to aggravate crosses and sufferings for each other. For it is the Father's will for us all to be happy and to love each other even in hard times.

(Our Father, 10 Hail Marys, Glory Be, »O my Jesus . . .«)

THE FIFTH SORROWFUL MYSTERY: You commended Your spirit to the Father and died on the cross after You had taken the cup given to You by the Father, because You were ready to accept it. I remain speechless here. I shall keep silent before Your cross! (I remain in silence for a while meditating on the event on Calvary.) There is nothing to be said here but only heave a sigh. O, is it possible that human wickedness can go so far? Is the love of God for us so strong that the Father did not even spare his own Son but allowed him to be crucified for our salvation. Is the Father's forgiving love in His

Son so great that he pardoned everyone immediately? My Jesus, thank You for having done all this for us. Do teach us to love and to forgive. Strengthen all those who, for the lack of their own love, cannot forgive, and destroy each other in hatred. Help us all to accept the Father's will as You did, because it is the only way to salvation. We pray to You also for the dying: give them strength to commend their spirit to the Father in peace. Take them into Your peace, O Lord Jesus.

(Our Father, 10 Hail Marys, Glory Be, »O my Jesus . . .«)

CLOSING PRAYER: I shall sing or read slowly the following hymn:

> O sacred head surrounded
> by crown of piercing thorn.
> O bleeding head so wounded,
> reviled and put to scorn.

> Our sins have marred the glory
> of that most holy face.
> Yet angel hosts adore thee,
> and tremble as they gaze.

> The Lord of every nation
> was hung upon a tree;
> his death was our salvation,
> our sins, his agony.

> O Jesus, by thy Passion,
> thy life in us increase;
> thy death for us did fashion
> our pardon and our peace.

Jesus, may the meditation on Your passion and death, on Your acceptance of the Father's will and of the cup of suffering from his hand bring me closer to You. May it give me strength for my suffering and bring me closer to those suffering around me. Thank You for what You have done for me. May Your passion and death be always in my mind and heart. Amen.

THE GLORIOUS MYSTERIES:
THE LORD CARRIES ME TO A NEW LIFE

In the name of the Father . . .
I believe . . .

INTRODUCTORY PRAYER: I wish to glorify You, O God, for You conquered death in Your Son. Open my heart and enlighten my mind that I may be able to glorify You. That is all I am going to ask of You in these mysteries. Enlighten me that I may glorify You! Let my life be for Your glory and to the honour of Your Son whom you raised from the dead by the power of Your Holy Spirit, who lives and reigns in unity with You and the resurrected Saviour. Amen.

THE FIRST GLORIOUS MYSTERY: You rose from the dead gloriously, my Jesus, and so conquered death. Glory be to You, glorious Conquerer! Glory be to You for having opened our tombs and taken us out to life. Praise be to you in heaven and on earth. And let all that was doomed to death and destruction glorify You! Let the whole universe praise You!

I am glorifying You with the Church in this canticle.

(I read slowly and in deep contemplation):

Heaven, earth and the universe
Let them exult and sing for joy:
Look, the victory of Jesus
Conquered death and brought us back life.

The time of grace is coming back,
Salvation has dawned upon us.

With the precious blood of the Lamb
The sins of the world have been washed.

On this day of resurrection
A hope's dawning for us mortals:
After death – we all know well –
With Jesus Christ shall we all rise.

Let us sing happy all the time,
Exult in the Resurrected:
The new life will last for ever,
With Christ, Easter has dawned to all. Amen.

(Our Father, 10 Hail Marys, Glory Be. »O my Jesus, forgive us our sins, save us from the fires of hell and lead all souls to heaven, especially those who have most need of Your mercy.«)

THE SECOND GLORIOUS MYSTERY. I glorify You, O my Jesus, because You did not leave Your apostles in suspense but gave them joy with Your resurrection and appeared to them for 40 days. And then, before their eyes, You went to the Father and were seated at his right hand, for this place was due to You as the conquerer of death. You told the apostles to pray and to wait for help.

We are celebrating with joy
The feast of Jesus' ascension.
Behold, the glorious Lord Christ
Reigns the world at the Father's right.

A bright cloud lifted him high up
Taking him from disciples' sight.
But a living and steadfast faith
Can see him present everywhere.

He was tied with love bonds to us,
Our pains he in his heart does feel:
At Father's right he thinks of us,
And pleads for us before his face.

Let us praise Jesus the Saviour
Celebrating his ascension:
With him we were all lifted up,
Heaven is our eternal home.

(Our Father, 10 Hail Marys, Glory Be . . . »O my Jesus . . .«)

THE THIRD GLORIOUS MYSTERY: We praise You,
resurrected Victor, because You sent the Holy Spirit, the
Comforter, upon the apostles, who were praying with
Your Mother, and changed their life. Thank You for having
turned their fear into courage, their anxiety into peace,
the lack of their understanding into the power of testimony
to the ends of the world.

As every year, so does this time
The day of joy come to us
When the Spirit, the Comforter,
Descended on the apostles.

In the form of the blazing tongues
The fire of God flickered o'er them,
Filling their mouths with words of God,
And heating their hearts to a glow.

As many days after Easter
Did this event come to pass,
As many years it once did take
For Jew, the slave, to be set free.

And now, O God, we pray to You:
Bestow graciously upon us
The gifts of Your Holy Spirit,
which You are sending from above.

(Our Father, 10 Hail Marys, Glory Be, »O my Jesus . . .«)

THE FOURTH GLORIOUS MYSTERY: Praise and glory be to You, my Lord, for not having spared Your Mother in Your suffering. Thank You for the graces You bestowed upon her enabling her to share in Your redemptive act for which reason we are now glorifying her in her assumption. Thank You for having taken her, Your humble servant and our Mother, with body and soul, up into heaven. Thank You for opening in her a new way for us – the way of resurrection!

Like the bright dawn of a new day,
Like the blazing sun at midday,
Like the bright moon that shines at night
Mary was taken up to heaven.

The one whom Your bosom once hid,
The one You laid in a manger.
You're now watching in Father's glory
As the king of all creation.

O woman, blessed above all,
More than angels and all saints,
Hear the loud cheers of the whole world
And of the angels' choirs above.

(Our Father, 10 Hail Marys, Glory Be, »O my Jesus . . .«)

THE FIFTH GLORIOUS MYSTERY: Be praised, O my Lord, for having crowned Your Mother Mary Queen in heaven. Thank you Mary for having allowed the Lord to be glorified through you.

> You, paramount to all creatures,
> God's Mother, the Queen of heaven.
> Our Creator the most gracious,
> Exalted You above all creation.
>
> Your Son, lifted up on the cross,
> Redeemed the world with his blood.
> You, witness of his agony,
> Became the Mother of us all.
>
> We exult to You today,
> Congratulating Your glory
> Look graciously upon us all,
> Keep a watch over Your children.
>
> Glory to Father, the All-high,
> With the Son and Holy Spirit,
> For having amply favoured You,
> For the diadem on Your head.

(Our Father, 10 Hail Marys, Glory Be, »O my Jesus . . .«)

CLOSING PRAYER: Thank You, O Lord Jesus Christ, for my having been able, through these glorious mysteries of the Rosary, to feel the power with which You conquered death and sin. Thank You for the joy which You prepared for Your Mother by Your resurrection, for Your apostles, for the whole world, for all creation. Thank You for our not being delivered to death any more, but invited to a new life. Thank You that no one among men, of Your brothers and sisters, must end in death and darkness from now on, but rather in light and life. Let my heart sing You praise incessantly from today! Let the song of resurrection, the song of the fullness of life, the song of joy, peace and love never fade from my lips. Let it be so through the intercession of Mary whom You glorified and through whom the Father was glorified in the Holy Spirit who lives and reigns with You, Jesus, and with the Father for ever and ever. Amen.

THE ROSARY OF PEACE

Introductory prayer

Heavenly Father, I believe that You are the good Father of all people. I believe that You sent Your Son Jesus Christ to the world to conquer evil and sin, and to accomplish peace among all people, for all people are Your children and Jesus' brothers. And once we know this, every destruction and every defilement of peace is all the more pitiable and incomprehensible. Grant now that I and all those who will pray for peace, may pray with a pure heart so that You may answer our prayers and give us true peace of heart and soul; peace to our families, peace to our Church and to the whole world! Good Father, remove from us all weeds of disturbance and disorder and give us the joyous fruits of peace and reconciliation with You and with all men. We ask You this with Mary, the Mother of Your Son and the Queen of Peace. May it be so!

I believe . . .

The First Mystery: Jesus offers peace to my heart.

»I leave you peace, my peace I give you. I do not give it to you as the world gives peace. Do not be distressed or fearful.« (Jn 14, 27) Jesus, quiet my heart. Open my heart to Your peace. I have had enough unrest and anxiety. Jesus, I have been cheated thoroughly by false hopes, bruised all over by heavy blows, cut by sharp blades. I have no peace. I am easily overwhelmed by worries. I am easily affected by fear and mistrust. Too

57

often have I hoped to find peace in this world, but my heart is still restless. Therefore, Jesus, together with St. Augustine I ask You to appease my heart and let it find rest in You. Do not ever let the waves of sin overflow it. Be my rock and my fortress from now on. Come back to me and stay with me, You who are the only fountain of my true peace. Thank You for the consoling words recorded by Your dearest disciple: »I tell you all this that in me you may find peace. You will suffer in the world. But take courage! I have overcome the world.«

(Our Father, 10 Hail Marys, Glory Be, »O my Jesus . . .«)

The Second Mystery: Jesus offers peace to my family.

»Look for a worthy person in every town or village you come to and stay with him until you leave. As you enter his home wish it peace. If the home is deserving, your peace will descend on it.« (Mt 10, 11–13)

O Jesus, thank You for having thought of our families as well. Thank You for having sent out the apostles to spread their peace in families. Now I ask You heartily to make my family deserving of Your peace. Cleanse us of all sinful thoughts and deeds that Your peace may grow and come into bloom within us. May Your peace remove all anxieties, all conflicts from our family. Grant that Your peace may completely overwhelm us and that You, the Peacemaker, may always be the first member of our family. I also pray to You for neighbouring families. Let them, too, be filled with Your peace and we shall all be fine.

(Our Father, 10 Hail Marys, Glory Be, »O my Jesus . . .«)

The Third Mystery: Jesus offers peace to the Church and calls her to spread peace!

»If anyone is in Christ, he is a new creation. The old order has passed away; now all is new! All this has been done by God who has reconciled us to himself through Christ and has given us the ministry of reconciliation. We implore you in Christ's name: be reconciled to God!« (2 Cor 5, 17–19)

Jesus, I implore You to give peace to Your Church. Reconcile all that is stil unreconciled in her. Bless priests, bishops and the Pope that they may live reconciled and perform the ministry of reconciliation. Remove from Your Church every unreconciliation. Reconcile all those who are at variance in Your Church and who, with their mutual conflicts, scandalize Your little ones. Reconcile various religious groups. May Your Church, spotless and stainless, be steadily calm. Let her be the promoter of peace.

(Our Father, 10 Hail Marys, Glory Be, »O my Jesus . . .«)

The Fourth Mystery: Jesus offers peace to his people!

»Coming within sight of the city, he wept over it and said: 'If only you had known the path to peace this day; but you have completely lost it from view! Days will come upon you when your enemies encircle you with a rampart, hem you in, and press you hard from every side. They will wipe you out, you and your children within your walls, and leave not a stone within you, because you failed to recognize the time of your visitation.'« (Lk 19, 41–44)

Jesus, you wept over Your city and over Your people. You offered them peace, but they were deaf and blind, and did not either hear or see. Thank You for the love toward Your people. Please grant that I may know how to lead my people, my town, my village, my homeland to the good. I pray to You for every individual member of my homeland, for each of my countrymen, for all those who are in authority. Grant that they may not be blind but that they may learn and recognize what they are to do for the realization of peace. Let there be no more ruin in my people, but let them all become solid spiritual buildings which will shine with peace and joy. Jesus, give peace to my people. Give peace to every nation. Let everyone live in peace and let everyone proclaim peace.

(Our Father, 10 Hail Marys, Glory Be, »O my Jesus . . .«)

The Fifth Mystery: Jesus offers peace to the whole world!

»Promote the welfare of the city to which I have exiled you; pray for it to the Lord, for upon its welfare depends your own.« (Jer 29, 7)

Jesus, on the earth has long since been sown and now germinating the dangerous seed of wars and all kinds of conflicts. And I know quite well that my peace, too, as well as the peace of all people, firmly depends on peace in all countries and nations of the world. Therefore I ask You to root out, with Your divine power, the ill-fated seed of unrest and sin as the first cause of every disturbance. Let the whole world be open to Your peace. All people need You in their life's unrest, so help them all to find peace, to realize peace. Many nations have lost their character. Many live in fear of others who are stronger and richer. Many of the poor and the persecuted rebel, while many of the rich and the wanton vent their fury over them. Generally, there is no peace or hardly any. So, Lord, send us Your Holy Spirit that he may bring that original divine order into this human disorder of ours. Let the nations be healed of their spiritual wounds so that mutual reconciliation may be possible. Send to all nations the messengers and harbingers of peace so that everyone may realize the deep truth of what You once said through Your great prophet: How beautiful upon the mountains are the feet of him who brings glad tidings, announcing peace, bearing good news, announcing salvation, and saying to Zion, 'Your God is King!'« (Is 52, 7)

(Our Father, 10 Hail Marys, Glory Be, »O my Jesus . . .«)

Closing Prayer

O Lord, heavenly Father, give us Your peace! We ask this of You together with all Your children in whom You have planted the desire for peace and appeasement. We ask this together with all those who, in unspeakable sufferings, are sighing for peace. And after this life, which we have spent in restlessness for the best part of it after all, take us into the kingdom of Your eternal peace and love. Accept also all those who fell as victims of wars and conflicts. Accept also those who are looking for peace on wrong paths. We ask this through Christ – the Prince of Peace – and through the intercession of our heavenly Mother – the Queen of Peace! Amen.

everything for each other so that
et all fathers and mothers conse-
at they may be able to consecrate
s and daughters.

tection and strength!«

sus made his life a sacrifice

love one another as I have loved you.
his: to lay down one's life for one's
u do what I command you.« (Jn 15,

t each of us may be willing to
hbour.

greatest love by giving Your
t all the glory You had from
the form of a servant. You
be ready to live with and for
You did for us. Thank You
by selfishness, haughtiness,
nindedness in us.

and strength!«

onquered Satan by his

what to think of this, two men
Terrified, the women bowed to
do you search for the Living
s been raised up. Remember
alilee – that the Son of Man
en, and be crucified, and on

THE JESUS ROSARY

In the name of the Father . . .

Introductory Prayer

Jesus, my Saviour, I want to be together with You
now. You are my brother and my Saviour. You have
remained with me and because of me. Thank You. Grateful for Your life, Jesus, I give up my life to You now at the
beginning of this prayer. I leave all worries, all problems,
all that attracts me and so draws me away from You. I
renounce sin by which I used to destroy our friendship. I
renounce evil by which I used to jeopardize our communion. I lay aside at Your feet all I have, Jesus, and want to
be totally Yours and, together with You, the Father's.

Mary, no one knew how to be with Jesus as well as
you did, for he grew up and developed at your side. Be
with me now that I may know and be able to be with
Jesus. Mary, pray with me that the Spirit of Jesus may
descend upon me, that he may pray in me and repeat:
Abba, Father! Amen.

I believe . . .

The First Mystery: Jesus was born in Bethlehem.

»And so Joseph went from the town of Nazareth in Galilee to Judea,
to David's town of Bethlehem – to register with Mary, his espoused wife,
who was with child. While they were there the days of her confinement
were completed. She gave birth to her first-born son and wrapped him
in swaddling clothes and laid him in a manger, because there was no
room for them in the place where travellers lodged . . . The angel said
to the shepherds: 'You have nothing to fear! I come to proclaim good
news to you – tidings of great joy to be shared by the whole people.
This day in David's city a saviour has been born to you, the Messiah

and Lord. Let this be a sign to you: in a manger you will find an infant wrapped in swaddling clothes.' Suddenly there was with the angel a multitude of the heavenly host, praising God and saying. 'Glory to God in high heaven, peace on earth to those on whom his favour rests. (Lk 2, 4-7; 10-14)

Intention: Let us pray for peace! - (In these or your own words:) Jesus, be peace to us all. Remove the obstacles which divide us from each other. Make us the people of good will . . .

– 5 Our Fathers

(I pray deeply and slowly)

»O Jesus, be our protection and strength!«

The Second Mystery: Jesus helps and gives everything for the poor!

»As sunset approached, the Twelve came and said to him: 'Dismiss the crowd so that they can go into the villages and farms in the neighbourhood and find themselves lodging and food, for this is certainly an out-of-the-way place.' He answered them, 'Why do you not give them something to eat yourselves?' They replied, 'We have nothing but five loaves and two fish . . .' Then, taking the five loaves and the two fish, Jesus raised his eyes to heaven, pronounced a blessing over them, broke them, and gave them to his disciples for distribution to the crowd. They all ate until they had had enough. What they had left over and above filled twelve baskets. (Lk 9, 12-13; 16-17)

Intention: let us pray for the Holy Father, our Pope and for all responsible persons in the world! Jesus You loved the poor and gave them earthly bread. moreover, You offer heavenly bread to all who hungry and thirsty. Move the heart of our Pope an all responsible persons in the Church and in states they may help distribute the goods of the earth jus that all may eat their fill and leave some over and

– 5 Our Fathers

»O Jesus, be our protection and strength!«

with readiness to do they may be happy. L crate their life in love th themselves to their son

– 5 Our Fathers
»O Jesus, be our pro

The Fifth Mystery: J for us.

»This is my commandment: There is no greater love than friends. You are my friends if y 12–14)

Intention: let us pray tha lay down his life for his nei

– Jesus, You showed the life for our salvation. You le the beginning and took on invited us to do the same: to each other, up to the end, as for enabling us to love. Destr hatred, jealousy, and narrow-
– 5 Our Fathers
»O Jesus, be our protection

The Sixth Mystery: Jesus resurrection.

»While they were still at a loss over in dazzling garments stood beside them. the ground. The men said to them: 'Why One among the dead? He is not here; he h what he said to you while he was still in must be delivered into the hand of sinful n the third day rise again.'« (Lk 24, 4–7)

THE JESUS ROSARY

In the name of the Father . . .

Introductory Prayer

Jesus, my Saviour, I want to be together with You now. You are my brother and my Saviour. You have remained with me and because of me. Thank You. Grateful for Your life, Jesus, I give up my life to You now at the beginning of this prayer. I leave all worries, all problems, all that attracts me and so draws me away from You. I renounce sin by which I used to destroy our friendship. I renounce evil by which I used to jeopardize our communion. I lay aside at Your feet all I have, Jesus, and want to be totally Yours and, together with You, the Father's.

Mary, no one knew how to be with Jesus as well as you did, for he grew up and developed at your side. Be with me now that I may know and be able to be with Jesus. Mary, pray with me that the Spirit of Jesus may descend upon me, that he may pray in me and repeat: Abba, Father! Amen.

I believe . . .

The First Mystery: Jesus was born in Bethlehem.

»And so Joseph went from the town of Nazareth in Galilee to Judea, to David's town of Bethlehem – to register with Mary, his espoused wife, who was with child. While they were there the days of her confinement were completed. She gave birth to her first-born son and wrapped him in swaddling clothes and laid him in a manger, because there was no room for them in the place where travellers lodged . . . The angel said to the shepherds: 'You have nothing to fear! I come to proclaim good news to you – tidings of great joy to be shared by the whole people. This day in David's city a saviour has been born to you, the Messiah and Lord. Let this be a sign to you: in a manger you will find an infant wrapped in swaddling clothes.' Suddenly there was with the angel a multitude of the heavenly host, praising God and saying. 'Glory to God in high heaven, peace on earth to those on whom his favour rests. (Lk 2, 4-7; 10-14)

Intention: Let us pray for peace! - (In these or your own words:) Jesus, be peace to us all. Remove the obstacles which divide us from each other. Make us the people of good will . . .

– 5 Our Fathers

(I pray deeply and slowly)

»O Jesus, be our protection and strength!«

The Second Mystery: Jesus helps and gives everything for the poor!

»As sunset approached, the Twelve came and said to him: 'Dismiss the crowd so that they can go into the villages and farms in the neighbourhood and find themselves lodging and food, for this is certainly an out-of-the-way place.' He answered them, 'Why do you not give them something to eat yourselves?' They replied, 'We have nothing but five loaves and two fish . . .' Then, taking the five loaves and the two fish, Jesus raised his eyes to heaven, pronounced a blessing over them, broke them, and gave them to his disciples for distribution to the crowd. They all ate until they had enough. What they had left over and above filled twelve baskets. (Lk 9, 12-13; 16-17)

Intention: let us pray for the Holy Father, our Pope, and for all responsible persons in the world! Jesus, You loved the poor and gave them earthly bread. But moreover, You offer heavenly bread to all who are hungry and thirsty. Move the heart of our Pope and of all responsible persons in the Church and in states that they may help distribute the goods of the earth justly so that all may eat their fill and leave some over and above.

– 5 Our Fathers

»O Jesus, be our protection and strength!«

The Third Mystery: Jesus surrenders completely to the Father and does his will.

»Then Jesus went with them to a place called Gethsemani. He said to his disciples, 'Stay here while I go over there and pray.' He took along Peter and Zebedee's two sons, and began to experience sorrow and distress. Then he said to them, 'My heart is nearly broken with sorrow. Remain here and stay awake with me.' He advanced a little and fell prostrate in prayer. 'My Father, if it is possible, let this cup pass me by. Still, let it be as you would have it, not as I.' . . . Withdrawing a second time, he began to pray: 'My Father, if this cannot pass me by without my drinking it, your will be done!' . . . He left them again, withdrew somewhat, and began to pray a third time, saying the same words as before.« (Mt 26, 36–39; 42, 44)

Intention: We pray for priests and for all those who are called to serve Jesus in a special way all their life.

Jesus, as You surrendered to the Father's will even in the most difficult moments, grant grace to all priests and to all consecrated persons that they may persevere in doing the Father's will. Disperse their fear of the cup of their life. Let them turn all the bitterness and loneliness of life into the way of resurrection.

5 Our Fathers

»O Jesus, be our protection and strength!«

The Fourth Mystery: Jesus knew he was going to give his life for us and did so freely, for he loves us.

»Jesus looked up to heaven and said: 'Father, the hour has come! Give glory to your Son that your Son may give glory to you, inasmuch as you have given him authority over all mankind, that he may bestow eternal life on those you gave him.' . . . I consecrate myself for their sakes now, that they may be consecrated in truth.'« (Jn 17, 1–2; 19)

Intention: Let us pray for families!

– Jesus, You loved us, that is why You went away to the Father so calm and resigned. Nothing was too difficult, for You were borne away by love for us. Fill our families

with readiness to do everything for each other so that they may be happy. Let all fathers and mothers consecrate their life in love that they may be able to consecrate themselves to their sons and daughters.

– 5 Our Fathers

»O Jesus, be our protection and strength!«

The Fifth Mystery: Jesus made his life a sacrifice for us.

»This is my commandment: love one another as I have loved you. There is no greater love than this: to lay down one's life for one's friends. You are my friends if you do what I command you.« (Jn 15, 12–14)

Intention: let us pray that each of us may be willing to lay down his life for his neighbour.

– Jesus, You showed the greatest love by giving Your life for our salvation. You left all the glory You had from the beginning and took on the form of a servant. You invited us to do the same: to be ready to live with and for each other, up to the end, as You did for us. Thank You for enabling us to love. Destroy selfishness, haughtiness, hatred, jealousy, and narrow-mindedness in us.

– 5 Our Fathers

»O Jesus, be our protection and strength!«

The Sixth Mystery: Jesus conquered Satan by his resurrection.

»While they were still at a loss over what to think of this, two men in dazzling garments stood beside them. Terrified, the women bowed to the ground. The men said to them: 'Why do you search for the Living One among the dead? He is not here; he has been raised up. Remember what he said to you while he was still in Galilee – that the Son of Man must be delivered into the hand of sinful men, and be crucified, and on the third day rise again.'« (Lk 24, 4–7)

»The seventy-two returned in jubilation saying, 'Master, even the demons are subject to us in your name.' He said in reply: 'I watched Satan fall from the sky like lightning. See what I have done; I have given you power to tread on snakes and scorpions and all the forces of the enemy, and nothing shall ever injure you. Nevertheless, do not rejoice so much in the fact that the devils are subject to you as that your names are inscribed in heaven.'« (Lk 10, 17–20)

Intention: Let us pray that sin may disappear, that Jesus may resurrect in us.

Jesus, conqueror of death, conquer sin and death in me. Conquer hatred in me and in others, that peace may come. By the power of Your word and by the power of a priest's word drive away the influence of Satan.

–5 Our Fathers

»O Jesus, be our protection and strength!«

The Seventh Mystery: Jesus ascends into heaven.

»Then he led them out near Bethany, and with hands upraised, blessed them. As he blessed, he left them, and was taken up to heaven. They fell down to do him reverence, then returned to Jerusalem filled with joy. There they were to be found in the temple constantly, speaking the praises of God.« (Lk 24, 50–53)

Intention: Let us pray that the will of God may be done and fulfilled.

Jesus, give us the Spirit of prayer and joy that we may testify to You with our life in every tribe and nation. Let Your Church be a permanent witness of Your immense love in the world.

– 3 Our Fathers

»O Jesus, be our protection and strength!«

The eight mystery: Jesus sends his holy Spirit upon the apostles and his mother Mary.

When the day of Pentecost came it found them gathered in one place. Suddenly from up in the sky there came a noise like a strong, driving wind which was heard all through the house where they were seated. Tongues as of fire appeared, which parted and came to rest on each of them. All were filled with the Holy Spirit. They began to express themselves in foreign tongues and make bold proclamations as the Spirit prompted them.

Intention: Let us pray for the outpouring of the Holy Spirit in his fullness on our families, on the whole church, on all the religious communities, on all the baptised, on all people, especially on those who decide on the fate of the world, that the Holy Spirit might inspire them good thoughts, good decisions and may he guide their steps towards peace.

Jesus, send us your Holy Spirit as you sent him upon your apostles and your mother Mary. May he continually inspire us, may he guide us, and introduce us into his truth. May he teach us love, and may he guide our steps towards peace.

7 Glory Be

»O Jesus, be our protection and strength!«

Closing Prayer

Jesus, it is good to be with You. Thank You! Thank You for Your life, for Your love of the Father and for Your surrender to the will of the Father. Thank You for having opened the way of salvation to us. Mary, help us to remain faithful on the way of salvation and to come into our eternal glory. Amen.

PRAYER BEFORE CONFESSION

In the name of the Father, and of the Son, and of the Holy Spirit! Amen.

1. Almighty, merciful and good Father! Here I am before You on my knees. I want to confess my sins and offences to You. Father, I am coming back to You like that prodigal son. I confess that I have sinned and that I no longer deserve to be called Your son. Kneeling before You, I beg You: Throw Your arms around my neck like the good father hugged his son who had squandered his money and ruined himself, and only then remembered his father's love. Father, look on me as You looked, through the eyes of Your Son Jesus Christ, on the woman sinner who stood before him, and he did not condemn her. Grant me the grace of contrition and of deep concentration that I may be able to stand in Your presence and to start a new life in the light of Your word!

Father, by the power of Your Spirit, take the hard stony heart out of my chest and give me, through this confession, a renewed heart, washed with Your love, healed with Your mercy! Cleanse my heart and soul that I may receive the ring on my finger as a sign of a renewed, strengthened bond! Give me the robe of peace and love and admit me again to Your table! Through sin I have broken off friendship with You.

Father, thank You for Your Son's having spoken to us about Your mercy in such wonderful parables!

»While he was still a long way off, his father caught sight of him and was deeply moved. He ran out to meet him, threw his arms around his neck, and kissed him. The son said to him, 'Father, I have sinned against God and against you; I no longer deserve to be called your son.' The father said to his servants: 'Quick! Bring out the finest robe and put it on him; put a ring on his finger and shoes on his feet. Take the fatted calf and kill it. Let us eat and celebrate because this son of mine was dead and has come back to life. He was lost and is found.'« (Lk 15, 20–24)

Father, grant me grace that I may feel the joy already now, while preparing to meet You in confession! Let every fear and hesitation disappear that I may know how to confess my sins. Send me Your Spirit that I may feel them, remember them. Give me the strength not to keep any of my sins secret, but to open my soul before You in simplicity and sincerity!

2. Mary, Mother of peace and reconciliation! You called us, as your children, to peace and reconciliation with the Father. Thank you that many here in Međugorje and in the world have heard your call and have come to be reconciled in a contrite holy confession. Thank you that many have found peace and inner freedom, because they responded to your call when you appeared with a cross and said through tears: Be reconciled!

O Mary, grant that, with your help, I may understand the horror of sin! Obtain by prayer the grace for me to weep over my sins and faults with which I stirred up unrest and hatred, defiled the Father's name, obstructed the coming of his reign, with which I destroyed joy, love and hope in others around me! Mother Mary, help me understand the depth of your Son's suffering which you witnessed! Grant that my heart may decide for the struggle against sin and sinful habits! My Immaculate Mother, help me return to the Father's house of togetherness and peace! Let the awareness of the responsibility for my own self and for others around me awaken within me, and especially for the plans the Father reveals through you!

I am sorry that your following words refer to me, too:

»Dear children ... You are still ready to commit sin and give yourselves up into the hands of Satan without thinking ...« (May 25, 1987)

I still sin and find excuses for my sin. I often blame others and think that they are responsible for what I do. Whenever I find an excuse for my evil deeds and my evil words, I know that I consciously collaborate with Satan who wants to keep me in sin, far from the kingdom of peace and love. Mary, obtain by prayer the power of the Holy Spirit that I may now, in silence, feel my sin and confess it!

3. Ask yourself in silence:

What are really my sins: hatred of others, unwillingness to be reconciled to someone, engaging in fortune-telling and sorcery, cursing, damning, blaspheming, and dirty language in general, negligence of prayer, neglect of holy mass, absent-mindedness in prayer and at Mass, disrespect for elders and superiors, drunkenness, killing, drugs...

Parents, especially, should ask themselves here whether they have killed unborn children by any form of abortion and whether they have confessed this sin. Let spouses ask themselves whether they have cheated on each other and whether they have really born as many children as they could have, whether they have lived their parenthood responsibly.

For the young especially: Do I endeavour to work, learn, study hard? If not, then I indulge in laziness and do not develop according to God's plan. I remain open to every evil, and so shall not be able, as a completely developed personality and expert, to contribute to the welfare of my family, community or society. And this is the most dangerous sin for us young, if we consciously or unconsciously resist the development of the gifts God has given us. This bears consequences for the entire life. Then, do I respect my parents and elders enough? Do I disturb the basic order in the family? Do I embitter the life of my parents and neighbours, instead of trying to make them happy?

Have I been spending too much time in front of a television set, watching films presenting immoral life, especially watching on purpose films which present sexuality and relations among people in an unbecoming manner? Have I played with my own body in a degrading manner bringing myself to sexual pleasure, especially inducing or seducing others into it? If I do this, I bring disorder into my life, which has bitter consequences for my future and the future of others. God has created me as a sexual being, but I have been called to grow in respect of my own self and of others that one day I could serve my life the way God wants it. If, in the evening, I read or watch worthless stuff, then I disturb the normal night's rest and open a way to mental illnesses. If I do so, I behave irresponsibly to myself, destroy myself and check my personal growth. This is exactly the secret of sin: it destroys me and does not allow me to grow positively!

I also ask myself: Have I been affected by haughtiness, greed, selfishness, laziness, or have I perhaps started to run excessively after material goods, neglecting spiritual ones? . . .

(Remain in silence and examination of your conscience until you have become quite aware of your sins and offences, of their danger to your life and to the life of others. Then pray!)

Heavenly Father, good and merciful, holy and worthy of my respect! You know my heart, my evil habits. In the light of Your love I see how I have misused Your goodness. Today I repent with my whole heart . . . I am sorry. Please, forgive me!

4. Mother Mary, you have come in the name of the Father and want to make me open to the Father's plans. You call me not only to leave sin, every evil and co-operation with evil, but also to teach me to co-operate positively with the Father's will. You want to encourage me by constantly assuring me that I am important for the plan of salvation. Therefore you have called me in the Father's name to grow in love every day and to bring peace to others. Our Lady, inspire my enthusiasm for co-operation in the plan of building my life and the life of the whole world, and it will be even clearer to me what sin means. Help me understand that it is not enough to keep a gift but that it must be developed. Help me discover the possibilities of co-operation with the Father's will, and through your intercession remove all obstacles in my way. Help me understand that I am responsible for the good I have missed in myself and in others.

Therefore, I do not only ask myself whether I have blasphemed and defamed God's name, but also whether I have always endeavoured to glorify his name, whether I have really prayed with the heart, finding time for prayer that it may be a true communion. I must seriously ask myself also how I prayed.

Have I really done good in every opportunity and loved God above all and every man as myself?

Have I tried to do something for peace on every occasion, or have I thrown obstacles in the way of peace?

If I was aware of the problems of this or that family, did I remain inactive, instead of helping with my prayers and fasting to bring peace to that family?

Have I resisted God's will consciously and thus remained half-hearted?

Have I helped others with my good example and words?

Have I given freely of my material goods? Or have I spent them on unnecessary things (cigarettes, make-up, newspapers, alcohol . . .), while I could have given them to the disposal of others for their daily bread?

Have i tried with all my heart to make good for the injustice I have done to others by hatred, jealousy, envy . . .?

O my God, merciful Father, thank You for my having understood that sin is not only an evil that I did, but also what I failed to do or could have done better. I promise to do everything to conquer sin and all evil habits in myself, to develop all that is good and positive in me and in others. Help me, Father!

Mary, be with me now and remain with me always so that my decisions may be real and firm!

5. Father, through Your son Jesus Christ grant, I pray to You, that all who confess here in Međugorje and in the whole world may come to know their sin, repent, make firm decisions and take the way of conversion and renewal of life! Jesus, destroy evil through every confession: my personal evil, the evil in our families, in the Church and in the whole world. Let the grace of reconciliation spread and bring spiritual and physical health and healing to everybody. Let every confession ward off all trials and

Satan's traps from everybody. Let everybody come out of their unconscious collaboration with evil and come into full co-operation with You.

6. Jesus, You sent out Your apostles to go into the world and to forgive sins in Your name. Thank You for having given such power to men. Therefore I consciously pray to You for all confessors in the world, especially I pray to You for the priest who is going to hear my confession now and give me absolution of sins and reconciliation! I pray to You for N. (Mention his name!) Inspire him with Your Spirit that he may know how to console and encourage me, that he may know how to lead me on the way of spiritual growth and warn me of the obstacles I place in my path. Bestow on him the grace of love that he, too, may accept me in spite of my sinfulness. Grant that he may always be ready to dispense the grace of reconciliation!

7. Mary, keep all confessors and help them. You are the Mother of all priests, because you are the Mother of the First High priest. Father, I ask all this in the name of Jesus Christ, Your Son in the Holy Spirit with Mary, Your lowly servant. Amen.

Closing prayer

We adore You, O Christ, and we bless You; because by Your Holy Cross, You have redeemed the world.

Therefore, while the promise of entrance into his rest still holds, we ought to be fearful of disobeying lest any one of you be judged to have lost his chance of entering. We have indeed heard the good news, as they did. But the word which they heard did not profit them, for they did not receive it in faith. (Heb 4, 1—2)

In their affliction they shall look for me: »Come, let us return, to the Lord, for it is he who has rent, but he will heal us; he has struck us, but he will bind our wounds. He will revive us after two days; on the third day he will raise us up, to live in his presence.« (Hos 6, 1–3)

Father, over the tomb of Your Son I am meditating on the word You said to me through the prophet and the apostle. Here I am! Heal me! Raise me up that I, with all creatures, may give glory to Your new creation, the creation You started on the third day after the death of Your Son! Create me anew so that I may serve You completely and one day exult in You for ever!

Mary, with you I want to live every day in the hope that the promises given to our fathers through the prophets will be fulfilled in me as well. May it be so and let it be fulfilled in me and in all people! Amen.

PRAYER ON FAST DAYS

Our Lady's call:

"I would like the world to pray with me these days! As much as possible! To fast strictly on Wednesdays and Fridays; to pray every day at least the Rosary: joyful, sorrowful and glorious mysteries ..." (August 14, 1984)

O Lord God, Creator of all creation and my Creator! Today we give You thanks for having arranged the world so wonderfully. Thank You for having given fertility to mother Earth so that she bears us all kinds of fruit! Thank You for the food prepared from the fruits of the earth! Father, I rejoice in Your creatures, I rejoice in all the fruits today, and I thank You! Thank You for our daily food and drink.

Father, thank You for having made my body in such a way as to be able to use the fruits of the earth and so develop and serve You. Thank You, Father, for all those who, through their work, produce new life possibilities. Thank You for those who have much and give away to others! Thank You for all who are hungry for heavenly bread while eating this earthly one! Father, thank You also for those who have nothing to eat today, for I am convinced that You will send them help through good people.!

Father, today I decide to fast. In doing so I do not despise Your creatures. I do not renounce them, I only want to rediscover their value. I decide for fasting because Your prophets used to fast, because Jesus Christ fasted and so did his apostles and disciples. I especially decide for fasting because Your servant, Mother Mary fasted, too. She called me to fasting:

»Dear children! Today I invite You to start fasting with the heart. There are a lot of people who fast because others do so. Fasting is a habit nobody wants to give up. I ask the parish to fast out of gratitude that God allowed me to stay in this parish so long. Dear children, fast and pray with the heart! Thank you for having responded to my call!« (September 20, 1984)

Father, I present this day of fasting to You. Through fasting I want to listen to and live Your word more. I want, during this day, to learn to be turned more toward You, in spite of all the things that surround me. With this fast that I take upon myself freely I pray to You for all who are hungry and who, because of their hunger, have become aggressive.

I present You this fast for PEACE in the world. Wars come because we are attached to material things and are ready to kill each other because of them. Father, I present to You this fast for all those who are totally tied down to material things so that they are unable to see any other values.

I ask You for all those who are in conflict because they have become blind in what they possess. Father, open our eyes, through fasting, to what You give us, to what we have!

I am also sorry for the blindness which has taken hold of my senses so that I do not give thanks for the goods I have. I repent every misuse of material goods because I used to judge their value wrongly. Make me able, through this fast today, to better see You and the people around me! Enable me to hear Your word better! Through today's fasting, let love for You and for my neighbour grow in me!

Father, I decide to live on bread and water today that I may better understand the value of heavenly bread, the presence of Your Son in the Eucharist. Let my faith and trust grow through fasting!

Father, I decide for fasting and accept it because I know that in this way my longing for You will grow in me. Eagerly and with gratitude do I think of Your Son's words: »How blest are the poor in spirit: the reign of God is theirs.« Father, make me poor before You. Grant me grace that through fasting I may understand how much I need You! Grant that through fasting my desire for You may grow, that my heart may long for You as the deer longs for the running waters and the desert for the clouds of rain!

Father, I pray to You, grant that through this fast my understanding of the hungry and the thirsty, of those who do not have enough of material goods, may especially grow! Help me see what I do not need but possess, that I may give it up for the benefit of my brothers and sisters!

O Father, I especially pray to You, grant me the grace to become aware that I am but a pilgrim on this earth, that, when passing away to the other world I shall not take anything but love and good deeds! Let the awareness grow within me that even when I possess something I cannot call it my own for I only received it from You to manage it. Father, grant me grace that through fasting I may become humbler and more willing to do Your will! So cleanse me of my selfishness and haughtiness!

Through this fast cleanse me of all bad habits and calm down my passions, and let the virtues increase in me! Let the depth of my soul open to Your grace through this fast so that it may totally affect and cleanse me!

Help me to be always like Your Son in trials and temptations, to resist every temptation, so as to be able to serve You and seek Your word more and more, day after day!

Mary, you were free in your heart and bound to nothing except the Father's will. Obtain by prayer the grace of a joyful fast for me today, in which my heart will be able to sing with You a thanksgiving song! Obtain by prayer the grace for me that my decision to fast may be firm and lasting! And I offer, for all people, the difficulties and the hunger I am going to feel today. Mary, pray for me! Let every evil and Satan's temptation keep away from me today through your intercession and through the power of your protection! Teach me, Mary, to fast and to pray that day after day I may become more and more similar to you and to your Son, Jesus Christ, in the Hoily Spirit! Amen.

THE ADORATION OF CHRIST IN THE MOST BLESSED SACRAMENT

1. Holy, holy, holy, Jesus in the Most Blessed Sacrament. Yes, holy and all-holy are You, Jesus. You are silently present in a simple small piece of bread. You are in front of me. Grant that I may understand with the heart that You are alive here for me and because of me! Fill me with living faith that You are here and that I am before You! O, grant me grace that I may adore You this evening with all my being: soul, spirit and body!

O, all you saints and angels, be here now! Adore the living Lord Jesus Christ with me! Mary, Mother of my Saviour and Mother of us all, be with us, too. You called me to adore and assured me that I would not be alone at this moment before your living Son. Thank you for this message:

»This evening, too, dear children, I am grateful in a special way that you are here. Adore the Most Blessed Sacrament all the time! I am always present when the faithful are adoring. Special graces are received then.« (March 15, 1984)

O Mary, thank you for your presence!

Like St. Thomas I would like to say this evening: My Lord and my God! I am not asking You, Lord Jesus, to hold out Your hands with wounds for me. I believe that You are alive here and that You are really present with the fullness of Your life and love. I remain in silence before You . . .

(Keep silent and meditate!)

Our Father, Hail Mary, Glory Be . . .

(Then sing this or some other Eucharistic song!)

Holy, holy, holy; holy and all-holy, Jesus in the Most

Blessed Sacrament . . .

2. Jesus, You are my God. You are the fountain of holiness and holiness itself. Only to You is my adoration due, to nobody else. Therefore I leave all things, all persons, all programmes. I leave everything and adore You. I want my heart and my mind to become one with You. I give myself up to You with all my being.

Mother Mary, I feel how unworthy I am to adore Jesus. Thank you for being with me! You were worthy of adoring and loving him more than anybody else in the world, because you are his Mother, loving and faithful. So, Mary, to you do I give my heart that you may adore Jesus in me and with me. To you do I devote my family, my friends, my community, my people and my Church.

O my Mother, I love you immensely and offer myself to you. Through your goodness, love and grace, save me! I want to be yours. I love you endlessly and I want you to protect me. I ask you, Mother of goodness, from my whole heart, to give me your goodness that I may be able to love everybody as you loved Jesus Christ! And I also ask grace of you that I may be gracious to you. I present myself completely to you and want you to be with me at every step, for you are full of grace. Amen.

Jesus, I have devoted myself to Your Mother now, that I may more fully belong to You. Grant that I may be Yours with her, as she was Yours! Look on her love! Grant that I may love You all the days of my life as she loved You! Remove from my heart every haughtiness, selfishness and all that is in the way of my adoring You deeply!

(Remain in deep silence!)
Our Father, Hail Mary, Glory Be . . .

(Eucharistic song!)

3. Jesus You loved me unto death and beyond it. You were born for me, You lived for me, You died and rose for me. When You realized that death would separate You from me, Your love was inventive: You remained with me and for me in the Most Blessed Sacrament. O be praised, Jesus, in this simple bread, in this host! Be praised, You who are all-worthy of every praise and glory!

Praise and glory to the Father who sent You to give Yourself up to us and for us in this way! Praise and glory to the Holy Spirit who, through Mary's intercession, is crying for joy through me: Praise and glory forever and ever!

Therefore I adore You in every church in the world: Be praised and glorified in every host!

Be praised and glorified in every Communion in which I meet You. Be praised and glorified for all those meetings when I received You without being fully aware that You had come to me, the living and true God. Be praised and glorified for every moment which I have passed with You so far and which I am going to pass with You in the future! Be praised and glorified in all those who live in love, because they receive You and are inspired by Your love! Be praised also in all those who forget You, who do not adore You! Be praised also in all who oppose or persecute You! Be praised and glorified in all who receive You but do not think of Your presence, nor live on it, but come back from Holy Communion or Mass as if they had not met You at all! O, be praised and glorified because You are alive now and want to present everyone around You with love and fullness of life!

(Remain in silence and let these words echo in you.)

Our Father, Hail Mary, Glory Be . . .

(In case of a communal adoration, sing a Eucharistic song!)

4. Lord Jesus, let every word I say during this hour of adoration be in Your Spirit! Do not let them be empty words! Inspire me to understand Your word which You pronounced to draw me completely to You! You said You were the bread for our soul, for our life, for every hunger, but first and foremost for the hunger of love. Jesus, feed my soul, for I am adoring You!

»So that we can put faith in you«, they asked him, »what sign are you going to perform for us to see? What is the work you do? Our ancestors had manna to eat in the desert; according to Scripture, 'He gave them bread from the heavens to eat.'«

Jesus said to them: »I solemnly assure you, it was not Moses who gave you bread from the heavens; it is my Father who gives you the real heavenly bread. God's bread comes down from heaven and gives life to the world.«

»Sir, give us this bread always«, they besought him.

Jesus explained to them:

»I myself am the bread of life. No one who comes to me shall ever be hungry, no one who believes in me shall ever thirst.« (Jn 6, 30–35)

Attracted by Your word which applies to me as well, I am here, Jesus, beseeching You: Give me to eat, give me to drink! I am hungry and thirsty. Nothing else can appease my hunger or my thirst, for everything is transient, everything is deficient. Thank You for being an answer to my hunger and thirst!

(Remain in silence!)

Jesus, here I am kneeling in the name of all those who

are hungry and thirsty for truth, justice, love, reconciliation. I am kneeling in the name of all the children who are hungry for the motherly bread of love and of their parents' home. I am kneeling in the name of all the thirsty who, on the roads of this life, are seeking the drinks which make drunk and lead to death, not to life. O, bread of eternal life, I am kneeling before You in the name of all who are quarrelling and waging wars, who hate or persecute each other, who behave jealously toward each other because of earthly bread! Jesus, reveal Yourself to them as the eternal heavenly bread! Let them find You and feel Your presence so that they will no more wander about the world, beaten up with evil and sin. Jesus, the manna of the Father for us travellers and pilgrims through the desert of this world, I also pray to You for all those who are hungry for earthly bread, who work, but do not get a pay, because the stronger and the richer exploit them.

This evening, Jesus, I am kneeling before You. Let my heart plunge into Your presence and let Your life completely absorb me so that, from now on, I may be a sweetness to all who are seeking You, that I may never again embitter life for anybody! Let me become the bread of life with You!

(Silence)

Our Father, Hail Mary, Glory Be . . .

(A Eucharistic song!)

5. Jesus, the bread of life, the life of the world, incomprehensible secret, the Father's Word to us all, I am at peace with You. Now, I am meditating on another word of Yours which on one occasion was recommended by Your Mother:

»No man can serve two masters. He will either hate one and love the other or be attentive to one and despise the other. You cannot give yourselves to God and money. I warn you then: do not worry about your livelihood, what you are to eat or drink or use for clothing. Is not life more than food? Is not the body more valuable than clothes?

»Look at the birds in the sky. They do not sow or reap, they gather nothing into barns; yet your heavenly Father feeds them. Are not you more important than they? Which of you by worrying can add a moment to his life-span?

»As for clothes, why be concerned? Learn a lesson from the way the wild flowers grow. They do not work; they do not spin. Yet I assure you, not even Solomon in all his splendour was arrayed like one of these. If God can clothe in such splendour the grass of the field, which blooms today and is thrown on the fire tomorrow, will he not provide much more for you, O weak in faith!

»Stop worrying, then, over questions like, 'What are we to eat, or what are we to drink, or what are we to wear?' The unbelievers are always running after these things. Your heavenly Father knows all that you need. Seek first his kingship over you, his way of holiness, and all these things will be given you besides.

»Enough, then, of worrying about tomorrow. Let tomorrow take care of itself. Today has troubles enough of its own.« (Mt 6, 24–34)

(Silence!)

Be praised and glorified for ever, O my Lord, when You call me to You with such words! Yes, You are my master and teacher. I have no other, nor do I want to have one. I want to serve You and nobody else. Now here before You I leave all worries, and anxiety, and fear, and mistrust. I present to You all that worries me. For, it is hard to be bound and fettered, pensive and anxious . . . And You offer me, in Your love, the freedom of birds and the beauty of lilies in the field . . .

Because of my own worries and plans I have no time for my friends, nor for anybody else. Could anybody give me a greater promise than Yours that You would take care of everything?! O God, You want me to be like a child from morning till night, to live happily, in joy and in total abandonment, not worrying my mind about anything.

After these words I still wonder whether it is possible at all. Yes, it is possible, for You say so, Jesus, and I shall understand it when You become my everything and when You are above all for me.

O Jesus, who would not give You glory, who would not adore You?! I cannot but pray to You day and night! Jesus, if it is so, let me understand, so that You may always be my everything!

(Silence!)

Our Father, Hail Mary, Glory Be . . .

(Sing!)

Have we trials or temptations? Is there trouble any where? We should never be discouraged: Take it to the Lord in prayer.

(From the song »What a friend we have in Jesus«)

6. Jesus, You said You had come because of the sinful and the sick. Thank You that, in Your holiness and

excellence, You do not turn away from us. Thank You for having forgiven me my sins and shared Your bread with sinners! Thank You for not having feared the criticism of those who considered themselves righteous and despised others as sinful and unworthy! Therefore I am praying to You now to forgive my sins, as well and to cleanse me completely!

Thank You, Jesus, for having sent out every Christian to be ready to do the same: to love without any conditions, especially where no reward is expected. Kneeling here before You, I decide for Your way and ask You to make me worthy to pray in Your name for my own cleansing and healing! Even more I thank You for being ready to heal others and bring them back to Your friendship through me! Jesus, make me worthy!

Mary, Mother of every consolation, be now with me and pray with me that from this moment I may be whiter than snow and that I may be able to work for the benefit of all those for whom I now want to pray to your Son with you.

(Mention by name those you want to pray for! Remain in silence!)

Our Father, Hail Mary, Glory Be . . .

7. Jesus, now my heart is joyful. I know that You will take care of me and of all people, my brothers and sisters. At the end of this adoration I promise that from now on I shall care more for You and for Your word. I shall endeavour – through prayer, meditation and adoration, through fasting and confession – to experience Your love and to pass it on. I know that my journey is still long, the destination still far. But thank You for the hope burning in my heart and for the love which has blazed up toward

You, and at the same time toward my brothers and sisters!

Jesus, I pray to You, make Your abode in me through Holy Communion! Grow and develop within me! Heal my soul and body! Keep me safe from every mental and physical illness, from every incurable and infectious disease!

Likewise, I beseech You to cure all the sick and the infirm! Glorify Yourself in all of us! Let Your face shine on the whole world through us!

Mary, be also with me! You are the Mother of Emmanuel, which means the Mother of God who decided to be with us forever.

Our Father, Hail Mary, Glory Be . . .

(At the end, sing!)

> Humbly let us voice our homage
> For so great a sacrament;
> Let all former rites surrender
> To the Lord's New Testament;
> What our senses fail to fathom,
> Let us grasp through faith's consent!
>
> Glory, honour, adoration
> Let us sing with one accord!
> Praised be God, almighty Father;
> Praised be Christ, his Son, our Lord;
> Praised be God the Holy Spirit;
> Triune Godhead be adored! Amen.

V. You gave them bread from heaven.
R. Having all Sweetness within it.

Let us pray!

O God, who in this wondrous sacrament have left us a memorial of Your passion, grant us, we beseech You, so to venerate the sacred mysteries of Your Body and Blood that we may perceive within us the effect of Your redemption. Who live and reign world without end.

R. Amen.

Blessed be God . . .

(The closing song!)

ADORATION OF THE HOLY CROSS

In the name of the Father, and of the Son, and of the Holy Spirit. Amen.

We adore You, O Christ, and we bless You; because by Your Holy Cross, You have redeemed the world.

1. Jesus, I fall on my knees before Your cross. Before the cross on which You died out of love for me. By it You obtained eternal salvation in heaven for us, and opened the way of peace and reconciliation on earth. Thank You for Your cross! Thank You for having carried it with love!

Jesus, I admit to You right away that I do not understand why You had to suffer. Therefore, all the greater is my gratitude to You for Your cross. Thank You for having marked me with the sign of the cross from the very beginning. At baptism this sign of salvation was indelibly imprinted into my soul and heart. Although I do not understand Your cross, it is neither a folly nor a scandal for me, but a sign of Your love and the way of my salvation.

Jesus, Your Mother, brave and faithful, was standing under Your cross. She was listening and taking to heart the words You uttered at the moment of Your terrible passion and death.

Mary, thank you for having carried the cross yourself. Thank you for having called me to stand by the cross and before the cross and to devote myself to it!

»Dear children! I want to tell you that the cross should be in the centre these days. Pray especially before the cross, from which great graces come. Now make a special consecration to the cross in your homes! Promise that you will not offend Jesus, or the cross and inflict insults on Him. Thank you for having responded to my call!« (September 12, 1985)

Here, Mary, at the beginning of this adoration, at your word, I devote myself to the cross. Be with me now and let this devotion be complete!

O cross, I consecrate myself to you. I renounce every sin against you and every sin in the world. I renounce every insult I have inflicted and which others have inflicted. I am ashamed, Jesus, of having sinned, of having offended You and the sign of my personal salvation. But from today I belong only to Your cross. Let it be the only sign of hope and salvation for me!

(Silence in front of the cross!)

Our Father, Hail Mary, Glory Be . . .

(Sing!)

> Cross of Jesus we adore you,
> our whole life we give to you,
> we dearly love you.

2. Jesus, Your cross is not a mute sign, but a cry for forgiveness, a cry for reconciliation of men to God the Father, a cry for universal justice and love. You were not silent on the cross. The suffering did not close Your mouth nor twist it with revenge, but it opened at the hardest moment and sought forgiveness and love!

So thank You for having pronounced the words of forgiveness when You most had a reason to condemn! Thank You for having asked Your Father for forgiveness and mercy at the time of crucifixion!

Father, thank You for having heard the words of Your Son, when Your fatherly goodness was »tested« because of the Son's suffering! Thank You, Father for his having pronouced the words:

FATHER, FORGIVE THEM; THEY DO NOT KNOW WHAT THEY ARE DOING!

Jesus, none of the men, especially those who were preparing Your death, had expected such words. Misled by hatred and endless darkness, they vented their anger on You by nailing You to the cross. They made fun of You. And You prayed to the Father not to punish them for their deeds.

Let these words now echo in my heart!

(Keep repeating to yourself: »Father, forgive them; they do not know what they are doing!«)

Jesus, scenes of cruelty are vivid in my mind. What cruelty of men! You did only good and this is how You are repaid. I am sorry that something like this could happen. Grant me tears that I may start crying before Your cross, which is a sign of our human cruelty and attraction to evil, but even more a sign of Your love for us!

Mary, you also experienced all this and heard His words of forgiveness. Thank you for having appeared to our visionaries with a cross in your hand, crying and repeating the words: PEACE! PEACE! PEACE!

I want these words to echo in my heart now. Let them inspire repentance and the desire for reconciliation in me!

(Remain in deep meditation and repent of your sins, especially the hatred and intolerance around you!)

Jesus, grant that this evening I may receive the grace of forgiving through Mary! Forgive me both when I know and when I do not know what I am doing! Cure me of my wickedness, that peace and forgiveness may enter deeply into me!

(Silence!)

Our Father, Hail Mary, Glory Be . . .

(Song!)

> Forgive me, my God, I repent, forgive me!
> Look, in sorrow my heart is dying!

3. Jesus, in Your cross I see Your endless love. You gave everything for us men, for Your brothers and sisters. You loved us even to the point of a humiliating death. You entered into the deepest levels of human suffering. You suffered endlessly. Although You carried the cross with love, You were not spared the deep pain. I cannot say, »It was easy for You to forgive because You are the Son of God.« It was not easy for You either, for You suffered without consolation, and that is the hardest form of suffering. You felt forsaken, lonely, helpless. That is why You gave that soul-stirring cry, »My God, my God, why have you forsaken me?«

Jesus, let these words enter deeply into my heart! Let them penetrate into the depths of my consciousness and subconsciousness! Let them wake me up and inspire full love and abandonment to the Father, for You emptied the cup of loneliness on my behalf!

(Keep repeating these words in silence!)

Jesus, forgive me that my love is not unconditional! Forgive me for having only sought my consolation and for having often so easily cried out to the Father, »Where are you, why do you not help, why do you not hear me?!« Forgive my distrust in the Father! So shallow and rootless is my word, »Father, Your will be done . . .!

Jesus, I pray to You for all those who are crying and moaning in their pain now, and do not doubt the Father's love but, resigned to his will, drink the cup of suffering and present it for the salvation of the world! Let love and trust grow in them through trials and tests . . .

Jesus, I pray to You also for all who have lost every trust in the Father because of suffering, and now do not pray nor seek Father's will, but live embittered, unreconciled to the Father and to men. Jesus, You experienced suffering. So, You do not condemn them but present their cries to the Father, asking him to forgive them, to appease them . . .

Mary, Mother of consolation, at the moment of deep suffering you could not offer consolation to your Son. You were helpless yourself, though not desperate but repeated the words once said in Nazareth. »I am the servant of the Lord, let it be done to me as you say.« Mary, when we do not know how to or cannot accept the Father's will, when we feel forsaken and misunderstood, be near our cross and say in place of us, »Father, here I am! I belong to You! I am Yours!«

(Silence!)

Our Father, Hail Mary, Glory Be . . .

> You have given me gifts without number,
> but, alas, I am a careless creature!

4. Father, before the cross of Your Son Jesus Christ I give You thanks for all his words from the cross! I know You heard them . . .

Mary, thank you for having accepted your new mission so whole-heartedly, when Jesus said to you, »Woman, there is your son!« Thank you that your heart had grown so ripe in love through suffering and pain so that your Son, at the moment of his death, entrusted to you all those he had given his life for on the cross! In this way, Mary, you gave birth to all of us under the cross. O brave Mother, thank you for not having feared pain and the cross! Thank you for having deserved such confidence . . .

(Remain in silence and listen in your heart to Jesus' words: »Woman, there is your son!«)

My Jesus, what a consolation it must have been for You that Your Mother bore patiently her cross following You on Your way of the cross! Now I pray to You for all who are lonely, who have become withdrawn, who have nobody, or who have been abandoned . . .

Jesus, I pray to You especially for the children who have been abandoned by their parents who in their selfishness forgot those they had given life to . . . I also pray to You before the cross for the children whom their mothers kill before they are born . . . Mary, be a Mother to all! I know that you are faithful and will not run away, that You are courageous; I know that you will always find a word of consolation in suffering, a word of joy at the moment of sorrow, a word of light at the moment of darkness. And I know, when you are not able to say the word, you will still be a Mother, for you took your Son's words seriously. Therefore, thank you also for the following words:

»Dear children! I, your Mother, love you and want to encourage you to prayer. I am tireless, dear children, and keep calling you even when you are far from my heart. I am a Mother, and although I feel pain for each who has gone astray, I forgive easily and I am happy about each child that turns to me. Thank you for having responded to my call! (November 14, 1985)

Our Father, Hail Mary, Glory Be . . .

> Under the cross the Mother stood
> Watching her Son nailed to the wood,
> With bitter tears in her eyes.

5. Jesus, You did not become blind in suffering, nor did hatred close Your eyes, because Your love and the sense of mission were divinely strong. You did not fall into darkness, because the divine light You bore in Your life was stronger than darkness. Thank You, therefore, even more now for having taken care of a disciple, and through him of us all, when You said: »Woman, there is your son!«

How beautiful and moving are these words which You addressed to the disciple You loved specially, asking him to take care of Your Mother, now his Mother! O how did these words echo in the ears of Your beloved disciple, now brother! What else could he do but say in his heart with joy, with deep responsibility and with responsible gratitude: »Yes, She is my Mother, when You said: 'Son, there is your Mother!'« So from that hour onward he took her into his care.

My Jesus, I can hardly imagine what a deep bond of love and togetherness was established and made firm between You, Your Mother and Your disciple at that moment. Thank You for having consciously realized the Father's plan! With the cross and under the cross, the beginning of a new mankind is realized . . .

Mary, thank you for having accepted the new son and in him all of us . . .! John, thank you for having accepted Mary as Mother in our name from that moment onward! Mary, I accept you, too.

(Silence!)

I know that a bond, born in suffering, is stronger than any blood relationship. Therefore, Jesus, I pray to You now for all our families where the links between parents and children, between brothers and sisters have broken, where unity has disappeared.

(Pray for a family you know is in difficulty.)

I pray to You, Jesus, also for all our monastic communities, and for all spiritual movements, and for the whole Church. Let our spiritual communities be born and renewed by the strength of togetherness born in suffering . . .

Our Father, Hail Mary, Glory Be . . .

In Your heart there is enough space for all people,
for You have come to all, that all may come to love You.

6. Jesus, divine sufferer, You are bringing to an end Your deed of salvation on the cross, Your mission. You finished it in the midst of the deepest pain and the rage of evil and sin. All the rage of hell, all the darkness of the world had come down upon You, but You remained divinely dignified and could say, »Now it is finished! Father, into your hands I commend my spirit!« The Father received Your spirit. And after the horrible cry on the cross the door of heaven was opened again to all who want it, even to the criminal on the cross. Thank You, my divine brother and friend, for having taken upon Yourself such pain and agony for my sake! Jesus, let Your death cry arouse my consciousness and subconsciousness so that I may tear myself away from evil and sin, from dissolute living and hatred, from darkness and hell, and to be open to the light!

Mary, obtain by prayer this grace for me! I remain with you, Mary, in silence . . .

Jesus, I pray to You with Mary for my death's hour. Even now I consciously declare: »Father, into Your hands I commend my spirit! As early as now, Father, I give over to You my pain and fear at the moment of my meeting with You! Cleanse me that I may be able to meet You! Jesus, on that day take me to Your kingdom, as You did that criminal from the cross!

(Pray in silence!)

Jesus, I pray to You for those who are now at their death's hour and are going through a deep fear of leaving this world and of facing You. Show them Your love. Curtail their earthly sufferings, which breed despair, and turn them into a meeting of hope! Have mercy on the dying, You who died so devoutly . . . Mary, be with every dying person as You were with Your dying Son! Alleviate their pain of loneliness by Your gentle motherly presence!

Jesus, I also pray to You for those who are now sad, worried or disappointed because they are going to part with their dear ones. Open for them the gracious fountain of faith and hope . . . I especially pray to You, Jesus, for mothers with sick children in their arms at their last breath. Be a consoler to them with Your Mother Mary!

Our Father, Hail Mary, Glory Be, Eternal Rest . . .

> When my body is dead and still,
> Let my soul with Your glory fill
> To enjoy You for ever.

7. Jesus, they slashed and tortured Your body all over, but darkness and sin could not affect Your spirit and

soul. Now, in front of Your cross, I am standing personally, wounded in soul and body, and ask You for healing.

On the cross You forgave me. You said: »Father, forgive them; they do not know what they are doing!«

It is only an offer to me. It is not yet a received grace. For, as the penitent thief went to heaven, the other cursed the offer of forgiveness. Therefore, Jesus, I want to seek, and I am seeking, not only forgiveness but also the healing of my wickedness: Jesus, Son of David, have mercy of me!

My heart is restless. It seeks everything, yet has the least time to be before You. It is restless because it did not understand Your love. Move my heart that it may no longer wander but find inspiration in You who, by forgiving, opened an inexhaustible source of peace! Jesus, Son of David, have mercy on me and cure me of restlessness!

I know that You are the Master. You can do everything. You lowered Yourself to be closer to me. And I do not feel it. I remain cold or so easily offend You. O, cure me of bad tendencies! Jesus, Son of David, have mercy on me and cure me!

What discontent, revenge, ill humour and moroseness exist in me! How hard it is for me to forget insults! I bear a limitless revengefulness, and make life difficult for myself. O, cure me with Your mildness of all my bitterness! Jesus, Son of David, have mercy on me!

O Jesus, You prayed hanging on the cross. You prayed for me, too. But I have forgotten prayer in distress so many times and have instead blasphemed, cursed and despaired, for I have no strength to retreat to prayer,

Forgive me! Cure my spirit of prayer! Teach me to pray! Jesus, Son of David, have mercy on me!

It is not only I who am unhappy on this earth. Around me I see so many unhappy, dissatisfied people, in quarrels and conflicts. They often blame only You. But they cannot see their sin as the cause of their unhappiness, and so are not converted. It is individuals, families, monastic communities, the world who are unhappy. O Jesus, cure us all! Cure parents, cure the souls and hearts of the young, heal all the wounds which sin has inflicted! Jesus, Son of David, have mercy on us!

Jesus, cure me of every deafness! I especially ask You to cure me of deafness to the word You send me through Your Mother! Cure my parish community of the deafness! Jesus, Son of David, have mercy on us!

Prayer for Physical Healing

(It can be added before the final blessing)

Jesus, Your hands and feet were pierced, Your side was pierced only that You may cure us, that You may heal the body which was created as the temple of the Holy Spirit. Jesus, cure us by Your patience in suffering: cure the sick and their attendants of impatience! You know that patience is easily lost in suffering. Heal our love so that we may bear pain as You did. Jesus, Son of David, have mercy on us!

Jesus, You accepted a crown of thorns on Your head, You received blows. By Your wounds and the crown of thorns cure me of every headache. Jesus, Son of David, have mercy on me!

You closed Your eyes in order to restore our sight. Heal my eyes. Restore sight to the blind! Jesus, Son of David, cure me of my blindness!

Jesus, You were obedient to the Father. You heard His word and You glorified him with Your lips. Jesus, restore our hearing and speech: heal the deaf and mute! Jesus, Son of David, have mercy on us!

Jesus, by Your pierced hands and feet cure every paralysis! Cure all the hands which are clenched into fists! Jesus, Son of David, have mercy on us!

Jesus, they pierced Your chest and heart that You may cure us. Heal our sick hearts, our bad blood circulation, our sick blood! Heal gout! Jesus, Son of David, have mercy on us!

You suffered innocently. Therefore I pray to You for all those who suffer because of other people's inattentiveness, because others are stronger and without love. Heal them, Jesus, Son of David, and have mercy on them!

If it be the Father's will that my suffering and illness should remain, then I accept them now again, and ask for strength for me and for all sufferers. Jesus, Son of David, have mercy on us!

Mary, here we are by the cross with you. You know our woes, problems and pains. You know our anguish and physical suffering. O Mother of consolation, thank you that I am not alone! Thank you for your being with me in my crosses and sufferings! I stretch out my hand to you and devote my life to you so that I may remain by the cross of your Son.

Mother, you said to us:

»Dear children! I want to clothe you, day by day, in holiness, goodness, obedience and love of God, that you may with each day become more beautiful and more prepared for your Master. Dear children! Obey and live my messages! I want to lead you. Thank you for having responded to my call!« (October 24, 1985)

Mary, clothe us as a mother does and prepare, wash and clean us that we may be ready for our Master and for each other!

Our Father, Hail Mary, Glory Be . . .

> And the blessing of peace, love and mercy,
> the blessing of spiritual and physical health
> may descend from the cross now on me
> and on the whole world!

In the name of the Father . . .

THE WAY OF THE CROSS

Introductory Prayer:

Jesus, Your Mother has called us to meditate on Your passion and death, to honour Your cross. I am ready to follow You with Your Mother and mine on Your way of the cross with the love Your Mother once followed You with. I want to bear my crosses as You once did Yours. Grant that by You I may learn how to help others to bear their crosses and to rise after each fall.

Mary, I start now with you, following Jesus on the way of the cross. I am carrying my cross, the cross of my family, of the Church and the world. I want to shoulder every cross and to help everybody. You said to the members of the Međugorje parish: »You parishioners have a big and heavy cross, but do not be afraid of carrying it! My Son is there to help you.« I am sure you meant these words for me, too, in order to encourage me. Thank you. Amen.

The First Station
Jesus, Pilate condemns you to death.

We adore You, O Christ, and we bless you;
Because by Your Holy Cross, You have redeemed the world.

Pilate called together the chief priests and said to them: »You have brought this man before me as one who subverts the people. I have examined him in your presence and have no charge against him arising from your allegations. Neither has Herod, who therefore has sent him back to us; obviously this man has done nothing that calls for death.« (Lk 23, 14)

The just man perishes, but no one takes it to heart. Devout men are swept away, with no one giving it a thought. Though he is taken away from the presence of evil, the just man enters into peace .. Of whom do you make sport, at whom do you open wide your mouth, and put out your tongue? Are you not rebellious children, a worthless race? (Is 57, 1–4).

The reason why Christ died for sins once for all, the just man for the sake of the unjust, was that he might lead you to God. He was put to death insofar as fleshly existence goes, but was given life in the realm of the spirit. (1 Pt 3, 18)

Jesus, here I am now in front of You. You do not condemn me, You do not seek my guilt but want to wash me of it. Thank you. Now I am sincerely sorry for having condemned others so many times, spoken badly about my neighbours, for having passed in silence over the injustices and wrongs done to others.

Jesus, grant that from now on I may be completely Yours. I pray to You also for all those who do the devotions of the way of the cross climbing Krizevac, or in their churches or homes. Be merciful to them all! Take away the condemnations that bear on them and those they inflicted upon others! From now on let man stand in front of man like brother in front of brother. Do not let the just man perish any more. Let love and peace come to reign!

Mary, you heard the condemnation but did not condemn. Stand by my side and by the side of all your sons and daughters! Thank you for having said:

»Dear children! This evening I would like to invite you in a special way to perseverance in trials. Think how the Almighty suffers because of your sins even today. So when sufferings come, present them as a sacrifice to God. Thank you for having responded to my call! (March 29, 1984)

(In a short silence I present my crosses and sufferings to God.)

106

Our Father, Hail Mary, Glory Be . . .
Have mercy on us, O Lord!
Have mercy on us!

The Second Station
Jesus, You take the cross upon Your shoulders.

We adore You, O Christ, and we bless You;
Because by Your Holy Cross, You have redeemed the world.

Jesus was led away, and carrying the cross by himself, went out to what is called the Place of the Skull, in Hebrew Golgotha. (Jn 19, 17)

Yet it was our infirmities that he bore, our sufferings that he endured, while we thought of him as stricken, as one smitten by God and afflicted . . . But the Lord laid upon him the guilt of us all. Though he was harshly treated, he submitted and opened not his mouth. Like a lamb led to the slaughter or a sheep before the shearers, he was silent and opened not his mouth. (Is 53, 4.6b–7).

Jesus said to all: »Whoever wishes to be my follower must deny his very self, take up his cross every day, and follow in my steps. . . . What profit does he show who gains the whole world and destroys himself in the process? (Lk 9, 23).

Jesus, You voluntarily took up your cross, because such was Father's will at that moment. You allowed Yourself to be treated harshly so that we may avoid ill-treatment. I am sorry for having so many times shaken off my cross, choosing the easier way. I am sorry for having often evaded the cross of love and patience, and chosen the crosses of irreconcilability, hatred, selfishness, impatience. Now I realize that with my behaviour I often imposed heavy crosses on the shoulders of my neighbors. Forgive me! From now on I am willing to accept crosses the way You did . . . Now I forgive all those who, with their sins, burdened me so many times with heavy, too heavy crosses. I pray to You for those who insulted me, who did not love me, who did not forgive me my weaknesses and sins, but repaid my weaknesses and offences with evil. I forgive them. Please, forgive them, too!

Mary, now I understand better that you are with me. Obtain grace for me through your prayers that I may know how to accept and carry crosses! Thank you for having urged me to pray for love in sufferings:

»Dear children! In these days, while you are glorifying the Cross joyfully, I would like your cross to be a joy for you. Pray especially, dear children, that you may accept sickness and sufferings with love the way Jesus did. Only in this way shall I be able to grant you readily the graces and healings which Jesus allows me. Thank you for having responded to my call!« (September 11, 1986)

Mary, do not tire of teaching me how to accept and carry crosses!

Our Father, Hail Mary, Glory Be . . .
Have mercy on us, O Lord!
Have mercy on us!

The Third Station
Jesus, You fall the first time under the cross.

We adore You, O Christ, and we bless You;
Because by Your Holy Cross, You have redeemed the world.

To the weak I became a weak person with a view to winning the weak. I have made myself all things to all men in order to save at least some of them. (1 Cor 9, 22)

As evening drew on, they brought him many who were possessed. He expelled the spirits by a simple command and cured all who were afflicted, thereby fulfilling what had been said through Isaiah the prophet:

»It was our infirmities he bore, our sufferings he endured.« (Mt 8, 16—17)

108

Jesus, I am watching how You have fallen under the cross. I know that even voluntary crosses can become too heavy. You need not have fallen. You could have called hosts of angels and You would not have fallen. But You went the way of a suffering man. You became like us in all things but sin. Thank You, Jesus!

When I now think of the falls of my love, faith and hope I can only say: Forgive me! So many times have I put aside my cross and not wanted to carry it, so that others had to fall under it. Forgive me that my love has so many times been short of breath! And so have my faith and hope often given way to despair...

Jesus, thank You for not having given up Your way after the fall! Thank You for not having said to the Father, »I cannot any longer«, but You rose and went on! Jesus, give me strength that I may rise after every fall, and watch over me that I do not fall again.

I pray to You also for those I passed by and was not ready to help get out of their troubles. Jesus, grant them the favour to rise, and teach me to help others rise.

My Saviour, many from the whole world stood in front of this station making decisions that they would take care not to fall. Now they are again crushed by the crosses of suffering, sin and evil. Jesus, may Your mercy find them and help them to their feet.

Peace in the world has fallen under the burden of hatred. Justice and love have fallen under the burden of the anxiety for money and possessions. Many are so tied down to material goods that they do not care to rise. Jesus, You fell for all that they may all rise. Grant that we may all rise and proceed on the way of resurrection.

(Pray by name for someone who you think is in great troubles!)

Mary, you helplessly watched the fall of your Son. But your presence and your faithfulness were certainly a great consolation to him. Thank you for promising to be with us, too.

»Dear children! No, you do not know how much grace God is giving you. You do not want to be moved these days, when the Holy Spirit is acting in a special way. Your hearts are turned to earthly things, and they engross you. Turn your hearts to prayer and ask for the outpouring of the Holy Spirit on you! Thank you for having responded to my call!« (May 9, 1985)

Mary, move us that we may rise with our crosses and be healed by the fall of your Son!

Our Father, Hail Mary, Glory Be . . .
Have mercy on us, O Lord!
Have mercy on us!

The Fourth Station
Jesus, You meet Your faithful Mother Mary.

We adore You, O Christ, and we bless You;
Because by Your Holy Cross, You have redeemed the world.

»Come, all you who pass by the way, look and see whether there is any suffering like my suffering, which has been dealt me when the Lord afflicted me on the day of his blazing wrath . . . He left me desolate, in pain all the day . . . At this I weep, my eyes run with tears: far from me are all who could console me, and who might revive me« (Lam 1, 12 . . .16)

»This child is destined to be the downfall and the rise of many in Israel, a sign that will be opposed – and you yourself shall be pierced with a sword – so that the thoughts of many hearts may be laid bare.« (Lk 2, 34–35)

Mary, you met your Son on the Way of the Cross. All you could do was to give him a consoling look. You

110

certainly could see it in his eyes that he had accepted suffering and the cross to save us. Mary, thank you for not having withdrawn! Love was stronger than bitterness and when your eyes met, you both accepted the Father's will again. You both suffer and carry the cross in love and devotion. Mary, obtain for me by prayer faithfulness like yours!

Jesus, forgive me for having avoided meetings with You, that they have often been superficial. Give me the grace of meeting You in every occasion!

I would like to meet others with love, too, both when I am suffering myself and when they are suffering. I do not want to run away from anybody again. Jesus, I also pray to You for all people who are suffering yet do not meet anybody who would be willing to help. I pray to You for all who are despised . . .

Jesus, I also pray to You for all those who perform these devotions on Križevac. Let them meet You. Please meet them, too. Let their life change and their suffering turn for their good and for the glory of the Father!

Mary, you have attracted many people to Križevac. Accompany them on their way as you did your Son. Let your motherly look meet every pilgrim that they may return home comforted and continue their life course in hope!

Thank you for the warning:

»Dear children! No, you do not know how to love and you do not know how to listen with love to the words I am giving to you. Be aware, my dear ones, that I am your Mother and that I have come to earth in order to teach you to listen out of love, to pray out of love, and not because and when you are forced to by crosses. It is through a cross that God is glorified in every man. Thank you for having responded to my call!« (November 29, 1984)

Mary, I decide to learn again to carry the cross with love and to meet with love those bearing their crosses . . .

Our Father, Hail Mary, Glory Be . . .
Have mercy on us, O Lord!
Have mercy on us!

The Fifth Station
Jesus, Simon of Cyrene helps You carry the cross.

We adore You, O Christ, and we bless You;
Because by Your Holy Cross, You have redeemed the world.

As they led him away, they laid hold of one Simon the Cyrenean who was coming in from the fields. They put a crossbeam on Simon's shoulder for him to carry along behind Jesus. (Lk 23, 26)

Rejoice instead, in the measure that you share Christ's sufferings. When his glory is revealed, you will rejoice exultantly. Happy are you when you are insulted for the sake of Christ, for then God's Spirit in its glory has come to rest on you. (1 Pt 4, 13–14)

My Jesus, those who had the task to torture You as much as possible and to crucify You as soon as possible, looked for somebody to help You carry the cross. And they forced Simon into it, a man coming to the temple for the Passover.

Simon, how did you feel? Did you not murmur to yourself: Why do I have to carry the cross for somebody who, according to our law, has deserved it? Do I have to share his disgrace? Simon, I understand your having resisted and murmured. But you still helped carry the cross for the one who knew how to find a way to say thank you. You helped Jesus carry the cross. We all call you blest Simon, for he certainly rewarded you with eternal life for that . . .

112

Jesus, thank You for having accepted this help!

Let me recognize you in every suffering man! Let me understand how I can be more blest than Simon of Cyrene because I can help you every day! Help me make use of every opportunity, so that I may enjoy the happiness of love already here.

Jesus, I pray to You for all those I did not want to help in their trouble! Forgive me, and cure them of their inflicted wounds!

Thank You for those whom I helped in Your name and who helped me in Your name! I pray to You also for all those who are helping readily today, because they love You and in You their brothers and sisters.

Jesus, many perform the Way of the Cross here and look for a Simon. Let them feel how You are close to them and let them go back home ready to carry each other's crosses and to share Your sufferings in this way!

Mary, thank you for your readiness to teach me to recognize and to love a brother or a sister in every human being. Thank you for reassuring me that I can help Jesus even today:

»Dear children! I invite you to help Jesus with your prayers realize all the plans which he is making here. Present your sacrifices to Jesus as well, so that everything may be realized as he has planned it, thus thwarting all plans of Satan. Thank you for having responded to my call!« (January 9, 1986)

Mary, with you do I present my prayers, and my sacrifices, and my life for the realization of the plans for love and peace in the world.

Our Father, Hail Mary, Glory Be . . .
Have mercy on us, O Lord!
Have mercy on us!

The Sixth Station
Jesus, Veronica wipes Your face.

We adore You, O Christ, and we bless You;
Because by Your Holy Cross, You have redeemed the world.

»Fairer in beauty are you than the sons of men.« (Ps 45, 2)

There was in him no stately bearing to make us look at him, nor appearance that would attract us to him. He was spurned and avoided by men, a man of suffering, accustomed to infirmity, one of those from whom men hide their faces, spurned, and we held him in no esteem. (Is 53, 2–3)

Answer me speedily, O Lord, my breath is at an end! Hide not your face from me, lest I should become like those going down into the pit . . . Let your face shine upon your servant! (Psalms)

Jesus, they also deformed Your face. Blood mixed with sweat. You could not be recognized any more. Your heart was the most beautiful, that is why Your face was beautiful. You were shining with Your inner beauty even at the hour of contempt and humiliation.

And then a courageous woman meets You and wipes Your face. Jesus, You do not forget to be grateful. Veronica found Your face impressed on her handkerchief . . .

Amid all the hostility toward You not everyone forgot that You had been doing only good, that so many times You had stopped the tears of bitterness and anguish, the tears that had run from pain and suffering. Thank you, Veronica, for not having been afraid although you were likely to meet with personal insults and humiliations because you had helped a condemned person.

Jesus, I am sorry for having so many times disfigured my own face and the faces of others with my sins, and knowing that You identified Yourself with us all. That means that I did the same to Your face. Forgive me, Jesus. You wanted my face and my life to be a reflection of Your face and Your life. But I have forgotten it so many times, so that Your light and Your joy could not reach others. Please, clean my face of every stain and wrinkle that Your light may shine forth from me, too.

I pray to You also for all those who had looked up to me for more love and understanding, but my look was obscured with selfishness and pride. Let Your face and Your light from now on shine forth in and through all of us!

Thank You for all those who today are helping Your most spurned brothers and sisters and also You in them!

Jesus, I especially ask You to help my people get rid of blasphemy with which so many defile Your face and Your name, Your honour and Your glory. Forgive and give new graces!

Mary, in your heart you thanked Veronica for her little favour to Jesus. Mary, obtain by prayer a great gift from your Son for me and for all pilgrims that his face may be reflected in our faces! This is your wish, too:

»Dear children! Today I invite you to decide whether you are willing to live the messages I am giving you. I want you to be active in living and conveying the messages. Dear children, I especially want you all to be a reflection of Jesus which will shine to this unbelieving world which is walking in darkness. I want you all to be a light to all and to testify in the light. Dear children, you are not invited to darkness, you are invited to light. So live the light with your life. Thank you for having responded to my call!« (June 5, 1986)

Our Father, Hail Mary, Glory Be . . .
Have mercy on us, O Lord!
Have mercy on us!

The Seventh Station
Jesus, You fall a second time under the cross.

We adore You, O Christ, and we bless You;
Because by Your Holy Cross, You have redeemed the world.

But I am a worm, not a man; the scorn of men, despised by the people. All who see me scoff at me; they mock me with parted lips, they wag their heads: »He relied on the Lord; let him deliver him, let him rescue him, if he loves him.« . . . I am like water poured out; all my bones are racked. My heart has become like wax melting away within my bosom. My throat is dried up like baked clay, my tongue cleaves to my jaws; to the dust of death you have brought me down. Indeed, many dogs surround me, a pack of evildoers closes in upon me. (Ps 22, 7–9. 15–17)

Jesus, after the comforting meetings with Mother, Simon and Veronica there followed a new fall. Certainly, heavier and more painful than the first one. Hatred and wantonness around You, the weaker they saw You, the more they raged, but You continued Your suffering and Your journey . . .

Thank You, O Jesus, for Your journey, for Your fall and for Your rising again!

Forgive me my falls, forgive me my decisions which were so short-lived! So easily did I forget my own journey and destination, and remained in evil habits. Jesus, now I want to rise again and I promise to rise whenever I fall. Thank You for being patient with me!

At this second fall of Yours, I pray for all those who have fallen and who have become disappointed in themselves and in Your mercy. Help them to rise. Let there be no more people who get stuck in sins and the troubles of life on their journey. Let a new strength and a new will for a fresh start flow through every heart!

Jesus, I pray to You also for those who have started a new life here in Međugorje, but have experienced the power of passion and bad habits and fallen again. Do not let them abide in sin! Let them accept their backslides in humbleness and simplicity! Do not let anybody be tempted beyond their own power.

Thank you, Mary, for these apparitions on account of which many have risen, because they felt your love. Let your appealing and comforting, and encouraging word echo in my heart.

»Dear children I invite you, the parish, to pray more during this time that still remains until the anniversary. Let your prayer be a sign of devotion to God! Dear children, I know you are all tired: no, you do not know how to abandon yourselves to me! Abandon yourselves completely to me these days! Thank you for having responded to my call!« (June 13, 1985)

Mary, I pray to you for this parish, for myself and for all pilgrims. Let there be no more fatigue, let love overwhelm every fatigue that we may again start walking with you . . .

Our Father, Hail Mary, Glory Be . . .
Have mercy on us, O Lord!
Have mercy on us!

The Eighth Station
Jesus, You speak a word to the women of Jerusalem.

We adore You, O Christ, and we bless You;
Because by Your Holy Cross, You have redeemed the world.

I will pour out on the house of David and on the inhabitants of Jerusalem a spirit of grace and petition; and they shall look on him whom they have thrust through, and they shall mourn for him as one mourns for an only son, and they shall grieve over him as one grieves over a firstborn. On that day the mourning in Jerusalem shall be as great as the mourning of Hadadrimmon in the plain of Megiddo. And the land shall mourn, each family apart . . (Zec 12, 10–12a)

A great crowd of people followed him, including women who beat their breasts and lamented over him. Jesus turned to them and said: »Daughters of Jerusalem, do not weep for me. Weep for yourselves and for your children. The days are coming when they will say; 'Happy are the sterile, the wombs that never bore and the breasts that never nursed.' Then they will begin saying to the mountains, 'Fall on us,' and to the hills, 'Cover us.' If they do these things in the green wood, what will happen in the dry?« (Lk 23, 27–30)

Jesus, gentle and humble of heart! Your passion did not make You either blind or deaf. You saw the women weeping for You and over You . . . You have never liked an insincere word . . . You, sufferer for all mankind, by Your passion and cross You did not want to arouse shallow compassion but to invite to a deep change of life. Thank You!

Jesus, forgive me for having looked for consolation where I could not find it! So many times have I overheard the truth and out of self-love turned to flatteries and lies. I did not have enough strength to say the truth with love. I deluded myself and others with my flattering words. Forgive all my insincerity and all my fear which induced me not to always seek truth in love! Help me that from now on I never look for false consolation, nor accept it or give it to others. I want to live my truth with others in Your light.

Forgive parents and all those who educate the young for having often closed their eyes before truth and for not having known how to convey it to others! Forgive also

Your whole Church for having often sought superficial solutions with this world, forgetting the thoroughness of love and forgiving!

Mary, thank you for the words I remember in front of this station:

»**Dear children I would like to guide you, but you do not want to listen to my messages. Today I call you to listen to the messages and then you will be able to live all that God tells me to convey to you. Open to God, and God will act through you and give you everything you need. Thank you for having responded to my call!**«
(July 25, 1985)

Our Father, Hail Mary, Glory Be . . .
Have mercy on us, O Lord!
Have mercy on us!

The Ninth Station
Jesus, You fall a third time under the cross.

We adore You, O Christ, and we bless You;
Because by Your Holy Cross, You have redeemed the world.

Where would you yet be struck, you that rebel again and again? The whole head is sick, the whole heart faint. From the sole of the foot to the head there is no sound spot: wound and welt and gaping gash, not drained or bandaged, or eased with salve. (Is 1, 5–6)

But he was pierced for our offenses, crushed for our sins. Upon him was the chastisement that makes us whole, by his stripes we were healed. (Is 53, 5)

The stone which the builders rejected has become the cornerstone. By the Lord has this been done . . . (Ps 118, 22)

Jesus, what else can I think before this repeated fall? I fall on my knees and observe with the heart what is happening to You. You are crushed to the end. Even those who were taking You to the place of crucifixion certainly became impatient because of Your falls, for these slowed down their plans. But You were patient both with Yourself and with them. You forgave them, Jesus, and presented Your wounds and bruises from the falls to the Father for us. Thank You!

Forgive me, Jesus, for having been impatient with the small and the weak so many times, while, at the same time, I feared the stronger, hesitating to support truth! Jesus, forgive me that my love has been weak so many times and has not dressed the wounds of others nor spared them from bruises. Therefore I pray to You for all those whose sins I have caused. Help them now!

I pray to You, Jesus, for all families crushed with the sins of parents, with the quarrels between father and mother, with the discords between children and parents, with doubts, blasphemy, alcoholism, killing of innocent life in a mother's bosom! Jesus, let them rise and take a new way!

I also pray to You for the young people who have become addicted to drugs and alcohol. Here, before Your heaviest fall I pray to You for the heaviest addicts who come and ask for Your help.

Jesus, become the cornerstone for all of us! Do not let us ever reject You so that our house may be safe! The world has rejected You in many things today. That is why many families break up and nations decay. O Jesus, be the cornerstone to us so that our walk with You may be upright.

Mary, you experienced this fall, too. A new sword of sorrow pierced your heart. You went on suffering and offering the falls for the new risings of us all. Thank you, O Mary, for the words which I now gladly recall:

120

»Dear children! Today I would like to tell you that God wants to send you trials which you can conquer by prayer. God tests you through everyday work. Pray now that you may calmly overcome every trial. Come more open to God out of all the tests and come to Him with love. Thank you for having responded to my call. (August 22, 1985)

Our Father, Hail Mary, Glory Be...
Have mercy on us, O'Lord!
Have mercy on us!

The Tenth Station

Jesus, You are stripped of Your garments and given sour wine to drink.

We adore You, O Christ, and we bless You;
Because by Your Holy Cross, You have redeemed the world.

And the soldiers (. . .) took his garments and divided them four ways, one for each soldier. There was also his tunic . . . (Jn 19, 23)

Put to death whatever in your nature is rooted in earth: fornication, uncleanness, passion, evil desires, and that lust which is idolatry. These are the sins which provoke God's wrath. Your own conduct was once of this sort, when these sins were your very life. You must put that aside now; all the anger and quick temper, the malice, the insults, the foul language. Stop lying to one another. What you have done is put aside your old self with its past deeds and put on a new man, one who grows in knowledge as he is formed anew in the image of his Creator ... Because you are God's chosen ones, holy and beloved, clothe yourselves with heartfelt mercy, with kindness, humility, meekness, and patience. (Col. 3, 5-10. 12)

Let us cast off deeds of darkness and put on the armour of light. Let us live honourably as in daylight; not in carousing and drunkenness, not in sexual excess and lust, not in quarrelling and jealousy. (Rom 13, 12b. 13)

Jesus, I am ashamed of what they did to You. They stripped You of Your garments. You remained without clothes, naked. You, divine Word, through whom all things were made and splendidly arrayed, stand. You allowed it in order to remove the curse of sin and death from us and to clothe us in the blessing of life and resurrection. Thank You!

Jesus, forgive me for having fallen to passions, for having indulged in the lusts of the body to the detriment of the spirit and the soul! Forgive me for having considered the needs of the body more important than the needs of the spirit. Give me the grace of conversion! Let Your grace change my old garments into new ones, so that from now on I may live according to the law of the spirit! Help me to put aside all vices: fornication, passion, greed, anger, wrath, malice!

Jesus, I ask the same from You also for those who come here. Let them go back home renewed. Let the laws of the spirit overpower the laws of the body, that they may be the witnesses of the new life which You won by Your passion and death. Let them all be clothed in the new garments of goodness!

Forgive every individual all the sins of impurity fornication and every kind of wickedness! Jesus, thank You for my being able to ask for all this with a renewed hope!

Mary, how you were feeling at this station, I cannot even imagine, let alone feel. I join now in your feelings and I want you to teach me to live by the spirit. Thank you for the word you said:

»**Dear children I want to clothe you, day by day, in light, goodness, obedience and God's love that you may be more beautiful and more prepared for your Master with every day. Dear children! Listen to and live my messages! I want to guide you. Thank you for having responded to my call!**« (October 24, 1985)

Mary, thank you for not putting up with the nakedness caused by my sin and thank you for the wish to clothe me in beautiful garments.

Our Father, Hail Mary, Glory Be . . .
Have mercy on us, O Lord!
Have mercy on us!

The Eleventh Station
Jesus, You are nailed to the cross.

We adore You, O Christ, and we bless You;
Because by Your Holy Cross, You have redeemed the world.

Indeed, many dogs surround me, a pack of evildoers closes in upon me; they have pierced my hands and my feet; I can count all my bones. They look on and gloat over me; they divide my garments among them, and for my vesture they cast lots. (Ps 22, 17–19)

Even when you were dead in sin and your flesh was uncircumcised, God gave you new life in company with Christ. He pardoned all our sins. He cancelled the bond that stood against us with all its claims, snatching it up and nailing it to the cross. (Col 2, 13-14)

O Jesus, the cross, which You have carried and which has bruised Your already wounded shoulders all over, now becomes Your hard bed. What pains You suffered while they were nailing You to the cross, nobody will ever be able to express . . .

Jesus, You opened a new way of salvation when You did not respond to insults, when You did not seek revenge for what they had done to You. Thank You, sufferer of all sufferers! Your suffering redeemed us men, because You loved in suffering and suffered in love.

Forgive me, Jesus, for having nailed others to the column of shame with my behaviour, for having driven others down to fear and anxiety with my anger, for having so many times nailed up the door of my heart with my hatred to keep others out. Redeem me from unjust desires and from evil habits which are crucifying me!

123

O Jesus, redeem the poor who are nailed to the crosses of poverty due to exploitation and the unjust behaviour of the rich! Redeem all the children who their parents are crucifying with their behaviour. Redeem, Jesus, from every crucifixion and tension between the state and the people.

Help us crucify every passion, every anger, every pride that peace and love, reconciliation and understanding may be born!

Mary, every blow echoed in your motherly heart. You endured it all. You remained upright. Thank you for loving me and for wanting to lead me to salvation! Mary, help me that everything within me that crucifies me or that I crucify others with, may be destroyed, so that from now on I may be crucified only by love for others! Thank you for this word of yours:

»Dear children! Today, too, I invite you to open more to God that he may act through you. As much as you open, so much fruit you shall receive. I want to call you to prayer again. Thank you for having responded to my call!« (March 6, 1986)

Our Father, Hail Mary, Glory Be . . .
Have mercy on us, O Lord!
Have mercy on us!

The Twelfth Station
Jesus, You die on the cross.

We adore You, O Christ, and we bless You;
Because by Your Holy Cross, You have redeemed the world.

If God is for us, who can be against us? Is it possible that he who did not spare his own Son but handed him over for the sake of us all will not grant us all things besides? (Rom 8, 31)

It was for this you were called, since Christ suffered for you in just this way and left you an example, to have you follow in his footsteps. He did no wrong; no deceit was found in his mouth. When he was insulted, he returned no insult. When he was made to suffer, he did not counter with threats. Instead, he delivered himself up to the One who judges justly. In his own body he brought your own sins to the cross, so that all of us, dead to sin, could live in accord with God's will. By his wounds you were healed. At one time you were straying like sheep, but now you have returned to the shepherd, the guardian of your souls. (1 Pt 2, 21–25)

Jesus obediently accepted even death, death on the cross. (Phil 2, 8)

Near the cross of Jesus there stood his mother Mary . . . (Jn 19, 25)

My Jesus, look to where love for us and obedience to the Father has brought You. Who of us will ever fathom Your love? So thank You for having loved us so much that we cannot even understand it! Let Your pierced heart be salvation for us all!

I want to be an answer to Your love. I kneel before Your cross, and want to hear and to listen to Your word with love. Let it enter into my heart as it did into the heart of Your Mother Mary who had strength enough to be by Your cross.

(Remain in silence!)

Heavenly Father, thank You for having entrusted Your Son Jesus Christ with such a commission! Thank You for his having accomplished it even unto his death on the cross! Thank You for having accepted his prayer to forgive us.

I also forgive all those who have insulted me. I pray to You for all those who do not forgive yet. Let Your mercy and the suffering of Your Son stir them to forgive so that peace may come to all men!

Mary, it was not easy for you to understand the Father's will but you accepted it together with your Son.

125

Thank you for having accepted us as your children. John, thank you for having accepted Mary in the name of all of us, and for having in that way expressed to her gratitude in our name! And thank you, Mary for your next call!

»**Dear children! I want to tell you that the cross is central these days. Pray especially before the cross, from which great graces come. Now make a special devotion to the cross in your homes! Promise that you will not offend Jesus or the cross and inflict insults on Him. Thank you for having responded to my call!«**
(September 12, 1985)

Our Father, Hail Mary, Glory Be . . .
Have mercy on us, O Lord!
Have mercy on us!

The Thirteenth Station
Jesus, You are taken from the cross and laid in Your Mother's arms.

We adore You, O Christ, and we bless You;
Because by Your Holy Cross, You have redeemed the world.

There was a man named Joseph, an upright and holy member of the Sanhedrin, who had not been associated with their plan or their action. He was from Arimathea, a Jewish town, and he looked expectantly for the reign of God. This man approached Pilate with a request for Jesus' body. He took it down, wrapped it in fine linen, and laid it in a tomb hewn out of the rock, in which no one had yet been buried. (Lk 23, 50—54)

Jesus, You ended Your life on earth in terrible suffering. You died as a hero of love and forgiveness. You commended Your spirit into the Father's hands. You took the criminal on the cross to heaven with You because he asked You to remember him. Jesus, thank You for Your coming to us! For every word, for every deed, for every sign by which You showed that You love us.

Mary! You were under the Cross. You heard everything, you suffered everything and now you are holding your Son in your motherly lap before his burial. With how much love and tenderness you took him from the cross, no one shall ever be able either to understand or to describe . . . (Mary, thank you for your warm motherly lap. Thank you for having taken him in your arms at the presentation and for having carried him in your bosom.)

Thank you for the Son of God having become man and our Saviour in your bosom! Thank you for your arms having received him even after men had killed him by nailing him to the cross. Thank you for your having committed him back to the earth with hope and faith!

Mary, now through you I ask for forgiveness of every sin which brought coldness into my heart spreading ice and chill all around. Thank you for being ready to take me into your motherly arms to comfort and lead me further on the way to the Lord!

Mary, I pray to you for all your children throughout the world. Especially for those who have grown cold, who sin has killed long ago, so that they are in the grip of death menaced by eternal death. Take them down from their crosses and let them come back to life by the power of God's Spirit!

Mary, I pray to you especially for abandoned children who do not know of the warmth of a mother's lap. Please be a mother to them, give them back the will to live! Mary, I pray to you for the mothers whose bosoms have become the graveyards of life, for they have either killed or abandoned their children. Restore them to life, too! Let the mother's bosom revive and do not let any become the grave but rather the cradle of life! Mary, thank you for the following words:

»**Dear children I have already told you that I have chosen you in a special way, just the way you are. I, the Mother, love you all. So have no fear of hard moments! Because I love you even when you are far from me and my Son. I beg you, do not let my heart weep bloody tears because of the souls who perish in sin! Therefore, dear children, pray, and pray, and pray! Thank you for having responded to my call!**« (May 24, 1984)

Mary, from now on I shall present you prayers for the salvation of all!

Our Father, Hail Mary, Glory Be . . .
Have mercy on us, O Lord!
Have mercy on us!

The Fourteenth Station
Jesus, You are laid in the sepulchre.

We adore You, O Christ, and we bless You;
Because by Your Holy Cross, You have redeemed the world.

A grave was assigned him among the wicked, and a burial place with evildoers, though he had done no wrong nor spoken any falsehood. (Is 53, 9)

And my body rests in peace and hope, carefree: because you will not abandon me to the nether world, nor will you suffer the Holy One of God to undergo decay and corruption. You will show me the path to life, fullness of joys in your presence, the delights at your right hand forever. (Cf. Ps 16, 9–11)

In baptism you were not only buried with him but also raised to life with him because you believed in the power of God who raised him from the dead. (Col 2, 12)

When the corruptible frame takes on incorruptibility and the mortal immortality, then will the saying of Scripture be fulfilled: »Death is swallowed up in victory.« »O death, where is your victory? O death, where is your sting« . . . But thanks be to God who has given us the victory through our Lord Jesus Christ. (1 Cor 15, 54–57)

Jesus, You accepted the cross, and death, and the tomb that You may be equal to us. By Your cross You consecrated suffering, by Your death You destroyed death, and by Your tomb You opened all tombs. Thank You. While I am standing over Your tomb, I am also thinking about my life and my end. I know neither the day nor the hour. But now again I give over to You my life and my death. I give over to You my fear of death, too. Let the moment of my passing away be consecrated by Your presence! Give me the consciousness that I always live in the light of this passage so that nothing in this world can stop or obstruct me on the way to You. Grant that I may find rest in the Father's bosom for ever.

I pray to You now for those who are dying natural death, prepared. I also pray for those who are dying a sudden death, especially a violent one, who are dying embittered and desperate. I pray to You for all those who find themselves with the dying. Let their presence be a help to them in death's hour! I also pray to You for those who are dying in an inhumane way: be close to them and take them into Your heaven! Save us all from eternal darkness! Bring us into Your light which shone forth over Your tomb on the third day!

Mary, be with me at the hour of my death! Take my life into your motherly lap! Mary, let me understand all that you have offered me here and live in joyful seriousness with you so that from now on I may do the Father's will every day as you did! Let every evil die within me and the good and life rise.

Thank you for this call:

»Dear children! Today also I want to call you to accept and follow the messages I give you with all seriousness. Dear children, it is because of you that I have stayed so long in order to help you realize all the messages I give you. Therefore, dear children, follow all the messages I give you out of love for me! Thank you for having responded to my call!« (October 30, 1986)

Our Father, Hail Mary, Glory Be . . .
Have mercy on us, O Lord!
Have mercy on us!

PRAYER ON THE SITE OF APPARITIONS

Mary, here I am, on your Podbrdo. Here I am, on the spot where the eyes of your chosen ones first saw you. Here I am, Our Lady, on the spot where you chose to start the great renewal of your children. Here I am, Mother of love, on the spot which you filled with your presence. Here I am, Mother of Peace, on the spot from where you, with a big cross in your hands, called everybody, through tears, to peace and reconciliation. I have come to be with you in this place. I want to say my »thank you« to you here on this rocky ground, in silence and solitude.

Thank you, Mother, for having come to us! Thank you for your special preference for the simple, the small and the lowly! Thank you for your motherly love and care that you show to us! Thank you for the hope and joy you gave us by your coming. Thank you for sharing our joy!

»Dear children! I thank the Lord again today for everything he gives to me, especially for this gift that I can be with you today, too. Dear children, these are the days when the Father is giving special graces to all who open their heart. I bless you and I want you, too, dear children, to recognize the graces and to put yourselves at God's disposal that he may be glorified through you. My heart carefully watches your steps. Thank you for having responded to my call!« (December 25, 1986)

Mary, thank you for having opened so many hearts and souls with your motherly love that they may put themselves at the disposal of God as you did!

Heavenly Father, I join Mary in saying to You: »Here I am, I am ready to do Your will! That is not difficult for me on account of the love and peace I feel here now. I open to Your word as the eyes of the visionaries opened at the moment of their gracious meeting with Your faithful

131

servant and our Mother.

Father, allow her to touch my life and my heart now again as she touched these rocks, brambles and thorn-bushes! My heart is often as hard as stone and prickly as brambles. Father, allow Our Lady to take me into her arms as she, on the second day of apparitions held a child in her arms, showing it to the visionaries from afar! Life has buffeted me all over. Let me find healing and appeasement in her bosom today again!

Mary, thank you for the experience of the visionaries on the second day of your apparitions! They were able to fly up here without having felt rocks and brambles. They were running to you and nobody could catch up with them. Our dear Lady, look how my step falters, how many times I am tired and burdened and cannot budge! I get stuck in trials too often and do not move on. My heart and my eyes are turned to the rocks and the brambles of life so that I cannot see a way through, and even if I start, I soon get tired and cut up. Today I have climbed your Hill. I did not come flying up like the visionaries did. But just because of that I all the more heartily ask you in this blessed place to make my steps through this world easier with your blessing. I put myself at your disposal, in all my weakness caused by sin and evil. Mary, thank you for your every descent by which you joined us all!

I pray to you also for all those who are still far away, who have fallen behind on the way, tired. Let them all feel the joy of your comings as you are happy about each of us! Let them move, let them be reconciled and overcome every rocky ground of life and find new ways of together-ness!

I pray to you, Mary, for the whole world, for all the responsible persons in all nations and states. Direct their hearts to peace! Bless them, too, that they may know how to bring others to the way of peace!

O good Mother, I want my heart to become totally obedient like yours, and cleansed, as yours has been since your Immaculate Conception. I also want to be in the light from now on, wrapped in the cloak of love and safety. I want, like you, to have every evil and sin under my feet. I want to crush the head of Satan. Mary, I want to be completely yours. Thank you for having said that you want to transform my heart, too, and to conform it to your motherly heart! I want to return home that way to other people, to my family, to the world.

And now I remain speechless. I only want to feel your love and presence with my heart and soul. I want to listen to the beats of my heart, leaning against a rock, as if I were in your bosom. Appease my heart that peace may enter into me . . . Bless me, Mother! Amen.

PRAYER BEFORE MASS

Heavenly Father, I give You thanks that I need meetings with You and men! Thank You that I have been created for togetherness and that the love of others makes me happy! Thank You for every friendly hand which helps me go through this life! Thank You for all the meetings in which I have felt that others are happy with me and in which I have prepared joy for others!

Special thanks to You for having made possible for me today's meeting with Your Son Jesus Christ who has remained for me in his holy Word and in the Eucharist, the sacred host. Thank You for his presence among us!

Jesus, I am eager to meet You in this Holy Mass. I am eager to hear Your Word. I am eager to receive You in the sacred host. You are my friend. I dare to come to You even when others despise me. Only You can appease my heart. Send me Your Spirit that I may understand what it means to live with You!

Mary, Mother, you have lived with Jesus every day for such a long time and so You know him best. Help me remove everything that is in the way of my meeting with him! Mary, thank you for having invited me to prepare for Mass like one prepares for meeting with a friend!

»Dear children! I would like to invite you to live Holy Mass. There are a lot of you who have felt the beauty of Holy Mass, but there are also others who come unwillingly. I have chosen you, dear children, and Jesus bestows upon you his graces in Mass. Therefore, live consciously Holy Mass and let your coming be a joyful one! Come and accept Holy Mass with love! Thank you for having responded to my call!« (April 3, 1986)

Mary, I want to live in the love which will be offered to me in this Mass, too. Obtain by prayer the grace for me that the word of your Son may move me, that his love may incite me to love, that his forgiveness may enable me to forgive! Let me be happy with the Mass every time just as you were happy over every meeting with your Son!

Jesus, remove all the burdens and loads from me that this Mass may be a spring of joy for having met You! Thank You, Jesus, for Your wish to meet me, too!

Jesus, forgive me for not having thought of You during Mass so many times because I was burdened with other meetings and things! Therefore, the meeting with You was without joy. Sometimes I did not know why I was there but You presented Yourself on the altar with undiminished love. Forgive me and take away my burdens so that this Mass may now be a real meeting with You!

Jesus, I pray to You also for the priest who is going to celebrate this Mass. Let his heart be ready to forgive everybody! Remove any burdens from his heart for this sacrifice and communion. Help him overcome the habit and routine, let every Mass be a meeting for him on which he will live and which he will readily make possible for others. I pray to You for the priests who have got into everyday worries and have no time to prepare for Holy Mass. Jesus, make their heart like the heart of all grace to proclaim Your word with joy, you whom they have experienced in their own heart!

(Pray with your own words mentioning the name of the priest!)

Jesus, I know how many of us could be here now at this Holy Mass. But many have stopped coming because of material worries and running after money, because they have broken off with You. Jesus, I can understand You, if You are sad. You come, You sacrifice Yourself and offer Yourself as food and drink but they remain far away, hungry, thirsty and tired. Jesus, I beseech You to send them grace that they may hear Your call, respond to it and come prepared for Your coming.

I pray to You for the young, too, whom You also want to meet. They also long for meeting You in the Holy Mass but do not come, and if they do, they do not know how to respond and are bored. Open their hearts also to the mystery of this communion that they may enjoy it!

Here, while I am preparing for this communion with **You, I recommend to You all my friends and acquaintances, especially the sick and the old who are not able** to come any longer. Jesus, let them meet You in those who have attended the mass! I present them all to You and come to this Mass in their name.

(Mention the names of the sick!)

Jesus, I also pray to You for the acolytes, the musicians, the singers and readers. Let them serve the alter with joy, let them sing joyfully and proclaim Your word! Let our hearts join in song and attentive listening! Let everything leap with joy because You are coming, You who are blessed forever. Let love fill all hearts, and sin and hatred disappear, that everything may burst into flower, for You give Yourself for us with all love! O grant that I may understand the mystery of Your sacrifice for us and profoundly bow before You with all creatures and the whole of heaven!

Jesus, let the love in my family, in my community and in the whole world grow stronger with this Mass!

Jesus, everything in my heart is ready for this meeting with You. Let all who are here with me now also be ready!

Let every soul be clothed in the whiteness of joy! Let every sin and its consequences disappear, that You may also be happy with us!

Come, Jesus, I am awaiting You! My longing for You has become deeper. Thank You for coming! Let this Holy Mass begin in Your name! Amen.

THANKSGIVING AFTER HOLY MASS

Jesus, after this joyful meeting with You send me out into the world again. You give me Your blessing and You do not leave me alone. You want me to bear the peace and love I have received here from You. Here I am, Jesus, I am ready to testify to You. Bless me! Bless also those I am going to live and work with today!

Jesus, You said we are the light of the world. Let your light kindle in my heart and grow so strong that no gale or storm, no passion or sin may ever extinguish it! With the light that I have received from You I want to inflame new lights, that there may be no darkness in relationships among people any more.

Jesus, You have offered Yourself to me in this Mass as the Way. Help me never to leave Your way and to follow it even more steadily I especially pray to You, on my way of the cross, make my patience stronger than impatience, my peace stronger than unrest, my love stronger than hatred!

Jesus, today You want to make use of my steps to be a friend and a guest to the sick and the weak. Here, bless my steps! Let these become the steps of peace and reconciliation, the steps by which You will be closer today to all who are lonely!

Jesus, I know that today You want to act through my hands. Consecrate and bless my hands that they may never reach out for evil or stretch a finger of accusation against others!

Jesus, with Your eyes You warned, expressed sympathy and called to love. Love and peace, mercy and righteousness, glowed in Your eyes. I consecrate my eyes to You today. Bless them that they may never be dimmed with the sin of selfishness and haughtiness! Let them never become eyes that boil with hatred and vengeance!

Jesus, Your heart beat for all men and brought warmth to everybody. Make my heart like unto Your heart now, so that through my heart, love may enter into my family and come to people I live with! Through my heart, Jesus, find also the sick that they may feel Your love! Make my heart like unto Yours that it may have more understanding for everybody!

Mary, you are my Mother. After meeting your Son in this Mass I want to go into life with you. Obtain by prayer for me the grace of testifying and conveying love as you called me:

»**Dear children! Today I call you to decide whether you want to live the messages I give you. I want you to be active in living and conveying the messages. Especially, dear children, I want you all to be Jesus' reflection which will shine to this unbelieving world walking in darkness. I want you all to be the light to everybody and to testify in the light. Dear children, you are not called to darkness but to the light. Therefore, live the light with your life! Thank you for having responded to my call!«** (June 5, 1986)

Mary, your wishes are my commands. Thank you for the promised help and for the confidence in sending me to others! Let the Father's will be done in me and through me! Amen.

PRAYERS FOR HEALING

(In Medugorje after the evening Mass, and elsewhere according to circumstances.)

Jesus, You came because of the sick and the sinful. Therefore, I turn to You and want to ask You to heal my soul and body. You know, Jesus, that sin tears and rips up the whole human being, that it destroys relations between people and with You. But there is no sin and no illness that You cannot drive away with Your almighty word. There is no wound You cannot heal . . .

Mary, you called me to pray for healing. Here, I want to do it now. So I ask you to accompany my prayer with your faith! Pray with me now that I may be worthy of obtaining by prayer the graces for me personally and for others who are sick and infirm!

1. Come, O Lord!

He got into the boat and his disciples followed him. Without warning a violent storm came up on the lake, and the boat began to be swamped by the waves. Jesus was sleeping soundly, so they made their way toward him and woke him: »Where is your courage? How little faith you have!« Then he stood up and took the winds and the sea to task. Complete calm ensued; the men were dumbfounded. »What sort of man is this«, they said, »that even the winds and the sea obey him?«

Jesus, You entered into the storms of the world. You also get into the boat of every life. You are present, for Your name is Emmanuel, God with us, God for us! So I am asking You now: Come into my life! The boat of my life also begins to be swamped, consciousness and sub-consciousness. Enter, Jesus, into the depths of my soul! I am lost! Stand up and tell my unrest to calm down, tell the death waves which surround me to stop threatening! Say the word to appease my heart that it may be able to hear Your divine, creative word!

(Remain in silence!)

Come, Jesus, into the boat of my family and of the whole world as well! Let our cries wake you up! Stretch out Your hand that calm may follow! Come, O Lord Jesus, come! Come to where I am most wounded . . .

Come, Jesus, also into those boats of life which stand anchored to bad habits, to drugs, to alcohol, to bodily pleasures, and do not move forwards! Jesus, calm the storms! Let everybody hear Your voice which brings peace!

2. Decision

Jesus, You are in my boat of life. You are my God, I adore You, I glorify You, for You alone are the Holy One, You alone are the Lord. I believe in You and I put everything at Your disposal with trust. I decide for Your love and Your mercy. With You and Your Mother I say: Let Your will be done to me in health and in sickness, in success and in failure, in joys and sorrows, in life and in death, in the present and in eternity.

Jesus, I have often been indecisive for the good, I have often done my will and so got slashed all over. Cure me of my unbelief and my resistances which I offered when I failed to understand the Father's will!

Mary, obtain by prayer the grace for me that my

decision may be a final one! Help me never to revoke it but to remain faithful!

(Silence!)

3. Renunciation

Jesus, I renounce every sin. I renounce Satan, and all his seduction, his lies and promises. I renounce every idol and idolatry. I renounce my unforgiveness and hatred, my selfish and haughty life. I give up all the wishes which caused me to forget the Father's will. I give up every spiritual illness and neglect that You, Jesus, may enter into my soul.

Mary, Mother, help me crush Satan's head in my life!

4. Prayer for Love

»You have heard the commandment, 'You shall love your country-man but hate your enemy.' My command to you is: love your enemies, pray for your persecutors. This will prove that you are sons of your heavenly Father . . .« (Mt 5, 43—44)

Jesus, You called to love . . . I admit to You that my love is weak. Cure me of the wounds of non-love and of all sins that prevent me from loving You above all, O my God! Cure my heart of the painful heritage I brought to this world because of the sins of the world and of my parents! Cure my soul of all burdens which have accumulated in me through my childhood and youth.

Let the fire of love, kindled by the grace of healing, destroy every darkness and completely melt the ice of evil in me! Enable me to love completely that I may love all men with my whole heart, even those who have insulted me. So often, Jesus, have I felt the inability of my love to forgive insults. Forgive my envy and jealousy that I used to burden myself and others with!

Heal my faith in You, too! Let the grace of trust remove every mistrust and every source of fear! Cure me of my godlessness in my thoughts, in my words, in my deeds!

Jesus, heal love in my family, too, so that it may be as it was in Yours! Heal love between spouses, between **children and parents, between the sick and the healthy...**

Jesus, heal love for all men throughout the world!

(Silence! Pray in silence for the person whom, at the hour of prayer, you do not love or whom you have not forgiven!)

5. Prayer for Healing of Soul

Jesus! Now I thank You for my soul, too!

All the consequences of sin reflect themselves in my soul, too. That is why I am often nervous and aggressive. I am often impatient and revengeful. Bad habits have settled in my soul, wounds and scars have remained, which makes my love of others more difficult. Certain experiences have settled to the bottom, often making me distrustful.

Jesus, cleanse my subconsciousness! Enter with Your light into my subconsciousness that darkness may never overwhelm it. With the power of Your grace touch those layers of my soul, too, in which the addictions to material things have settled which breed fear! Cleanse me that my spirit may be more open to You!

Heal me of mistrust in You and in Your word! Jesus, I beg You, heal me of all wounds and frustrations caused

**by failures and unfulfilled wishes. Cure me of every in-
ner darkness and heal the wounds in the depths of my**
subconsciousness! Let my subconsciousness calm down
in You, Jesus!

Now I pray to You also for all who are mentally ill and
encumbered. Take off their burdens and clean the
wounds which develop mental diseases! Keep the children who have inherited heavy mental burdens. Cure
every split personality, depression and fears, every neuro-
sis and psychopathic state!

Cure also all those who have become mentally ill due
to a failure in the family, at school or at work. Remove
from them the thoughts of suicide and free them from
every forced thought!

Jesus, be the Master of our souls! Cure all who have
busied themselves with suspicious practices! Deliver them
from every consequence of witchcraft and sorcery! Rest
every soul and restore peace to it!

6. Prayer for Physical Healing

»As evening drew on, they brought him many who were possessed.
He expelled the spirits by a simple command and cured all who were
afflicted, thereby fulfilling what had been said through Isaiah the prophet:
»It was our infirmities he bore, our sufferings he endured.« (Mt 8, 16–17)

Jesus, cure my body. Here I am before You with my
physical pains and the dangers threatening my body.
Cure me of the diseases which are affecting my body
now.

(Mention your own disease!)

Protect me from every disease!

If it is Your will for me to carry the cross of illness, then

I accept the cross and ask You for the grace to carry it with love. Jesus, now I pray to You for the healing of the members of my family and my relatives!

(Mention their names here!)

Jesus, I pray to You, if it is the Father's will for them to suffer, give them the strength to bear their crosses with love!

Cure all the sick in the world. Protect the world from epidemics and incurable diseases. Jesus, in one word, cure all our illnesses, for You came to take them upon Yourself and to save us!

Heavenly Father, thank You for having created me, for having redeemed me through Your Son! Thank You for healing my body, my soul and my love through him now. Let the blessing of peace and reconciliation, of love and trust pour out on me, on my family, on the whole Church and on the whole world. Let Mary, our Mother, obtain by praying together with us from Your fatherly goodness all that we need for soul and body.

May it be so! Amen.

WHEN YOU RETURN HOME

Dear pilgrim, Seeker of God! When you come to Međugorje, you are called upon to pray in the church, to celebrate the Mass, confess, adore Jesus in the most-holy Sacrament of the altar, then to pray on Križevac (the hill which reminds us of the passion and death of Christ as well as of our own suffering and our own cross) and on Podbrdo, the Hill of Apparitions. I believe that you have done that, that you have renewed your faith, love and hope and that you have felt how near God is. Anyway, that is exactly the reason for your coming here.

And really, God is very close here to all who are seeking him. You can feel his presence, you can come to love him. He gives us the strength to abandon ourselves to him. God has created here an oasis of PEACE through the Queen of Peace.

I am sure that there is a question now on your lips which bothers many pilgrims: It is nice here! It is easy here! Everybody is praying, everybody is seeking God. But at home? What can I do there for my peace to grow, for my love to develop? What can I do that trust may overcome mistrust, that the spirit of reconciliation may be stronger than non-reconciliation?! This question is of decisive importance.

Međugorje is what Tabor was for the disciples: to convince that it is possible to live love and to experience the glory of God, but then one has to return home, to one's own Jerusalem, to one's own everyday routine, to work, to school, among people who do not have the same conviction.

147

Yes, one has to return home!

In Međugorje you prayed for long hours. It was not difficult for you to climb Križevac no matter if the weather was good or bad. You also found time for Podbrdo. And you were fine.

Now leave Međugorje as a parish community and go back home. In your heart take along the places and events of Međugorje!

We know one thing: at home you have your own Križevac, your own hill of the cross, your own cross and suffering. You left it at home and it is waiting for you. But have no fear! The Križevac of Međugorje is not easier than your own back at home. Nevertheless, it has become understandable and bearable for many, since the lower hill, the Hill of Apparitions, became, by God's will, a place **of intensive communion with God through Mary. Therefore, although your Krizevac at home is standing and waiting for you, often built out of troubles and sufferings for which you are neither responsible nor to blame. Build a smaller hill next to it right away, build your own Hill of Apparitions, your own Tabor!**

Then Križevac, too, will get a new colour, will be wrapped up in new peace and new hope. Build the Hill of Apparitions in one corner of your flat or house! Furnish it with a smaller crucifix, a candle, the Bible, rosary beads **and a kneeler. There you will understand your Krizevac, too, and your passage, and your passing. By the side of** the Hill of Apparitions, Križevac becomes a place of resurrection, for no Križevac is there to destroy you, but to help you attain to salvation.

Remember well! Our Lady has taken Christ's words seriously. She goes with you up to your Križevac, up to your Calvary, like she said in a message for Christmas 1986.

Dear children! I thank the Lord again today for everything he gives to me, especially for this gift that I can be with you today, too. Dear children, these are the days when the Father is giving special graces to all who open their hearts. I am blessing you and I want you, too, dear children, to recognize the graces and to put yourselves at God's disposal that he may be glorified through you. My heart carefully watches your steps. Thank you for having responded to my call! (December 25, 1986)

This message does not refer only to those who are in Medugorje or only to the visionaries. It is addressed to me, to you, to everybody.

Go home, blessed forever by the Blessed forever!

And build an altar on which you start to offer your crosses and pains, woes and troubles, hope and joy, love and faith every day! Thus you will have your church, and your Krizevac, and your Podbrdo. Thus God will be with you, and Mary will carefully watch your step.

Go in peace! Bear peace and blessing!

WITNESSES: IVAN, MARIJA, IVANKA, JAKOV I VICKA IN THE MOMENT OF ECSTASY

*Ivan and Marija during an apparition
in the balcony of the Church.*

The evening Pilgrim Mass.

From Mt. Podbrdo looking toward Mt. Krizevac.

Climbing Mt. Krizevac, stopping to pray the Stations of the Cross.

Carrying the sick up the Apparition Mountain.

St. James Church

Mt. Podbrdo (Apparition Hill)